PRAISE F

AND THIS BOOK:

"In *Creating Your Own Happiness*, Yuri Choi reminds you that happiness, creativity, and freedom are available to all of us at any time. I highly recommend this book for anyone who wants to experience more clarity and peace and is serious about creating a meaningful life."

— Hal Elrod, Author of *The Miracle Morning* and *The Miracle Equation*

"Yuri Choi shares her wisdom and knowledge and reminds us all powerfully that it's never too late to start living a life full of purpose and joy becoming a beacon of light for others. She will remind you that you are the CEO of your own life!"

— Sharon Lechter, Best-selling Author of *Think and Grow Rich for Women*, Co-author of New York Times Bestseller *Rich Dad Poor Dad*, *Outwitting The Devil*, and *Three Feet From Gold*. Featured as one of the *World's Greatest Motivators.*

"I love Yuri's passion for positively changing the world. She inspires the reader through her inner wisdom and her joyful radiance. I am certain *Creating Your Own Happiness* will transform many people who wish to live meaningful lives."

— Frank Shankwitz (1943-2021), Co-Founder of Make-A-Wish-Foundation, Speaker, Author of *Wishman*

"*Creating Your Own Happiness* is a must read for anybody who wants a practical guide for living a happy life. Yuri has a way of igniting creativity and lighting up souls around her through everything she does, and the book captures her creative essence. She will reach many and touch your soul."

— Rob Angel, Founder of *Pictionary,* author of *Game Changers*

"Here's the deal...are you looking to create your own happiness and stop allowing other people to determine your future? Great, then read, embrace, and live by these amazing techniques that Yuri Choi brings to your life. It's a must read!"

— Erik "Mr. Awesome" Swanson, five times #1 Bestselling Author and Award-Winning Keynote Speaker

"In *Creating Your Own Happiness,* Yuri Choi shows us exactly how to grab a hold of the destiny we want and turn it into our reality. Part of that process is freeing ourselves from our limitations. Then we have room for expansion, and once that expansion begins, watch out! The question then becomes, 'How good can you stand it?' Let Yuri lead you down the path to that kind of happiness."

— Patrick Snow, Publishing Coach and International Best-Selling Author of *Creating Your Own Destiny* and *Boy Entrepreneur*

"Yuri Choi has known pain, but more importantly, she's learned how to turn around that pain to create happiness on her own terms. Every page of this book vibrates with truth, understanding, compassion, and the power of expansion. Embrace *Creating Your Own Happiness* and get ready to go on the ride of a lifetime!"

— Tyler R. Tichelaar, PhD and Award-Winning Author of *Narrow Lives* and *The Best Place*

WHAT YURI'S CLIENTS ARE SAYING ABOUT WORKING WITH HER

"I do not say this lightly, I have spent over $300,000.00 in education and coaching – I don't say this to brag, gloat, or to show people what I've done, but to say my investment in Yuri has been more impactful than all the other coaches I have ever had in my life."

— Hung Nguyen, *Entrepreneur*

"If you've already achieved a certain level of success in your business or work life, but you can't really figure out what's missing or why you're feeling empty sometimes, then Yuri will help you find that. She will help you find the missing puzzle piece to your emptiness."

— Tai Khuong, CEO of *Psych2Go,* largest mental health online magazine & YouTube Channel (with over 4.1 million subscribers)

"Before I started working with Yuri, my life was a crazy mess of stress and paranoia with absolutely no balance. My personal identity was my work and I neglected other parts of my life. After working with Yuri, today is a completely different story. I'm an active participant in my own life again. My wife said to me the other day, 'you just seem calmer and easier to be around.' Working with Yuri taught me how important it is to be present in all aspects of my life, build a balance, and look for the reflections of yourself in the world. Without this work, I know I wouldn't be living life, but rather living in fear of losing my identity. Since completing the course, I feel like the man I was years ago. Calm, confident, worthy of what the Universe is put in front of me. The biggest area of my life the work has affected is honestly... all aspects of my life.

Yuri helped me to see the possibilities in all aspects of my life and it isn't exaggerating to say it is life-changing."

— Austin M., *Project Manager*

"[Through working with Yuri] I've rediscovered the path back to fulfillment and contentment with life. I am pleased to say that I will end 2020 a better person than when I started the year, which was my goal going into our work together. When I show up to work the best version of myself, I show up as the leader that my team members deserve. I am engaged, positive, and having fun making an impact on people's lives. I can very confidently say that Yuri has helped a rather lost version of myself rediscover my passion for living life, both for myself and for others."

— Eric K., *Business Owner*

"Life was uninspiring and I felt like I didn't have a purpose before working with Yuri. I've struggled with self-confidence throughout my life, but after going through Yuri's coaching program, I can truly say I'm the most confident I've ever been. Yuri's program has changed my life through and through. To my surprise, we were able to tackle many different topics throughout working together, including repairing my relationship with my dad, building self-confidence, creating a vision, going through a career change, and finding purpose in life (to name a few). Things are going extremely well for me today. I feel confident in my life and career, and I'm excited to wake up every morning to take on the day. My relationships with family and friends have improved significantly, and many have commented that they love this 'new Aaron.' I genuinely feel I am a happier person, and as a result, I feel healthier and more fulfilled. Looking back, it was absolutely worth every penny.

What is completely changing your life for the better worth to you? I would highly recommend working with Yuri. As long as you truly want to change your life and have an open mind about it, Yuri will give you the tools and guidance you need to do it."

— Aaron T., *Entrepreneur*

"BY (before Yuri), I was struggling with sustaining my drive and concentration to do my work. I found myself distracted and being "busy" instead of being productive. I knew my work is where I am meant to be, but something was missing. This emptiness carried over into my personal life, where I was not being present and enjoying the precious time I have with my wife and my two daughters. Today I feel empowered. I feel energetic. I feel unstoppable after working with Yuri. If you are considering working with Yuri, stop considering and take the first step toward a better, happier you. It is without a doubt worth your time and investment."

— Anthony D., *Financial Advisor*

"I was in this cycle of being numb to feelings, and didn't really understand how important it is to have love and connection. I actually felt like I could truly be helped after my first conversation with Yuri. I knew I wanted to be this specific person, but didn't know how to get there. Yuri has helped me personally, spiritually, and business-wise. I am now on track to make $100,000 more this year from working with Yuri. I've referred many people to Yuri because this stuff works...it simply works. I would refer Yuri to anyone in any walk of life."

— Matt M, *Professional*

"Thank you, Yuri. You're opening my eyes—I've spent decades with them closed."

— Adam A., *Financial Advisor*

"Absolutely work with her. Yuri is an excellent coach and is there to support you 100 percent. She will listen, hold you accountable, and you will be a better person after spending time with her. I am very thankful that I participated in the program."

— Carl H., *Director of Finance*

"Yuri, you are a healer. You have gifts that manifest your devotion to wisdom and truth. You are wise beyond your years. I'm so thankful that the Universe brought me to you and nobody else. You possess everything that is good, wonderful, real, and beautiful."

— S.B., *Therapist*

"Working with Yuri has helped me gain my confidence again. Yuri helped me understand how my brain worked and to rewire some of the thoughts that I had. With this journey I was able to get back on track with my journey. I want today that I really appreciate everything that Yuri had done for me and for the help she has given me to find where I am today."

— H. Y., *Professor & Concert Pianist*

CREATING YOUR OWN HAPPINESS:

Your Practical Guide to Fulfillment, Inner Peace and Spiritual Freedom

YURI CHOI

Creating Your Own Happiness: Your Practical Guide to Fulfillment, Inner Peace and Spiritual Freedom

Published by:

Aviva Publishing

Lake Placid, NY

(518) 523-1320

www.AvivaPubs.com

Yuri Choi

Email: coachwithyuri@gmail.com

Website: creatingyourownhappiness.com

ISBN: 978-1-890427-35-1

Library of Congress Number: 2020916119

Editor: Tyler Tichelaar, Superior Book Productions

Cover Design: Shiloh Schroeder, Fusion Creative Works

Author Photo: Anthony Thai

Every attempt has been made to properly source all quotes.

Printed in the United States of America

"Go for it now.

The future is promised to no one."

- Dr. Wayne Dyer

Dedication

I dedicate this book to my father, Hyun Soo Kim (1947 - 2017):

Dad, can you believe it? I did it. My lifelong dream of publishing a book is happening. I can picture just how proud and excited you would have been for me. You always reminded me that I am a healer, that I am creative, and that I am loved. Thank you for teaching me to be present to all the blessings, to be a free spirit, to sing with joy on Saturday mornings, to be kind to all humans, to love unconditionally, to create, and to dream. Thank you for teaching me to listen to my soul and my heart. Thank you for believing in me. I know you're always with me. I love you. I miss you.

I dedicate this book to my mother, Soon Nam Lee:

Mom, I don't know how I got so lucky to have such a selfless, smart, resilient, strong, and beautiful woman as my own mom. There are not enough words in this entire world to let you know just how much I love you and what you mean to me. You always believed in my ability to write and inspire people since I was very young. Thank you for believing in me. I wouldn't be the woman I am today without you. I am incredibly thankful for you. I love you forever.

I dedicate this book to you, the reader:

It is my genuine hope that through the messages shared in this book you, it helps you find happiness, peace and success, even more.

Acknowledgments

AJ Mirhzad, Alec Stern, Amie Barsky, Andrew Solomon, Anne Sandoval, Anthony Thai, Bonnie Dimmick, Brené Brown, Brianne Grant, Brian Tracy, Dr. Bruce Lipton, Cameron Herold, Carlos Roman, Chandler Bolt, Charlie Houpert, Chris Pan, Christina Rendon, Chiara Mazzucco, C.G. Choi, Cori Coffin, Dan Clark, Dana Liesegang, Daniel Pink, Daniel Raphael, Deepak Chopra, Derek Doekper, Don Miguel Ruiz, Elon Musk, Eli Wilde, Elisa Huang, Ella Lee, Erik Swanson, Eric Kim, Esther Hicks, Frank Shankwitz, Gabby Bernstein, GwiShik Shin, Hal Elrod, Hafiz, Heidi & Ryan Blackstock, Dr. Hank Adler, HamIm Sun, Hojin Lee, Hussien Elbanna, Hyun Soo Kim, Jade Alectra, JaeHyung Lee, JaeKyu Lee, James Seriph, Dr. Jeffrey Fannin, Jeff Hoffman, JonKovach Jr., JooHyun Lee, Jungae Oh, Dr. Joe Dispenza, Kyungae Ko, Ken Walls, Les Brown, Les Brown, Lionel Lee, Lisa Nichols, Malcolm Gladwell, Martin Lee, Marianne Williamson, Mascha Zeer, Neale Donald Walsch, NeungHwan Lee, Noelle Lee, Oprah, Paul Wiggins, Patrick Snow, Patrick Carney, Paulo Coelho, Rachel Ivanovich, Dr.Rafael Luévano, Rhonda Byrne, Riadh Hamdi, Rick Hanson, Richard Mendius, Rob Angel, Robert M. Drake, Rumi, Sarah Snyder, Dr. Shari Young Kuchenbecker, Sharon Lechter, Shiloh Schroeder, Soon Nam Lee, Susan Friedmann, Stephanie Kosack, Steve Jobs, Mother Teresa, Tai Khuong, Thich Nhat Hanh, Tony Robbins, Tyler Tichelaar, Urpi Arriola, Dr.Wayne Dyer.

CONTENTS

Preface 1

Introduction 4

Part i: Accessing The Creator Within You 9

Chapter 1: Realizing You Are A Creator 10

Chapter 2: Creating Your Own Definition Of Happiness 18

Chapter 3: Creating An Unapologetic Life To Be Happy 25

Chapter 4: Accessing Clarity 34

Chapter 5: Creating Your Best Self Avatar 44

Chapter 6: Self-Leading Yourself 53

Chapter 7: Igniting Your "Why" 66

Chapter 8: Creating Your Destination As Your Best Self 72

Chapter 9: Creating Your Own Rules 76

Chapter 10: Accessing A Creator Mindset 82

Chapter 11: Activating Your Best Self 91

Part ii: Unleashing Yourself Towards Freedom 95

Chapter 12: Shedding The Masks 96

Chapter 13: Freeing Yourself From Judgments 105

Chapter 14: Honoring Your Truth 112

Chapter 15: Freeing Yourself From Perfectionism 116

Chapter 16: Being Present 123

Chapter 17: Detaching From The Illusion Of "Normal" 129

Chapter 18: Forgiving & Letting Go 134
Part iii: Expanding With The Universe 142
Chapter 19: Embodying Playfulness & Curiosity 143
Chapter 20: Embracing Your Failures 148
Chapter 21: Expanding Through Resilience 153
Chapter 22: Creating Abundance Through Courage 161
Part iv: Expression 170
Chapter 23: Leveraging Your Emotions 171
Chapter 24: Expressing Your Intentions 199
Chapter 25: Leading With Your Soul 203
Chapter 26: Expressing Gratitude 207
Chapter 27: Declaring Your Desires And Visions 216
Part v: Connection 222
Chapter 28: Connecting To Self 223
Chapter 29: Connecting With Others 231
Chapter 30: Connecting To Nature 238
Chapter 31: Connecting To The Idea Of Death 243
Chapter 32: Trusting In The Universe: Surrendering 252
Chapter 33: Owning Your Spirituality 258
A Final Note 266
About The Author 269

"Our deepest fear is not that we are inadequate. Our deepest fear is that we are powerful beyond measure. It is our Light, not our Darkness that most frightens us."

- Marianne Williamson

PREFACE

How to use this book:

First of all, you will notice that each chapter starts with a poem that is signed "y.c." This is my poet name that I've had for many years. I've picked out some of my favorite poems that I have written in the last 9 years to start each chapter for your soul. This will evoke deep thoughts and start to knock on your soul for deeper reflection and transformation to be had.

I hope this book serves you as your interactive and transformative guide towards your best version of yourself. To maximize the magic of this book, read one or two chapters a day then participate in the journaling exercises following each chapter. This is how the book is organized.

Part I of this book sets you up to create the transformation vehicle towards a happier, optimized version of yourself, the roadmap, and the tools necessary to create the pathway and guidelines as you shift to create and live a fulfilled life. This part of the book is a bit more systematic in nature, as it is there to set you up the structure needed to safely explore different ideas for the rest of the book.

Parts II through IV provokes insights and different perspectives about various subjects to explore after the structure has been created in Part 1, including freedom, expansion, and self-expression as ingredients for happiness.

The last part (Part V) ends with a spiritual inquiry and exploration. This part of the book will ignite you to think about how to create a relationship with the Universe and connect to self and the rest of the world in a meaningful way. The last part is intended to ignite some questions about spirituality that you've never considered before, as well as leave you with some to continue to ponder on.

This book is meant to be your companion, your practical guide, and your spiritual journal as you rediscover your authentic self. I hope that you get to redefine what it means to create happiness in your life. I envision that you will expand powerfully in this journey, if you engage in the exercises and the journaling prompts fully and apply the wisdom and knowledge I freely share here, in your own daily life and business. In this journey, transformation is absolutely possible, if you allow it. You will start to gain back that edge and spark in life and business, which you've lost. You will start to feel free again in ways that you haven't allowed yourself in a while. You will start to feel authentically confident again. You will start to believe you are truly unstoppable and infinitely capable of creating any reality that you desire. You will start to know and start to feel deep in your body that you are infinitely loved by the Universe. This process will grant you an immense amount of inner peace, if you surrender to the process. Perhaps you will start to live sharing more of your own gift that has been hiding within you. The magic to be unfolded through this book cannot be all predicted, and my intention is that this book leaves you with some to many refreshed perspectives about how to live a more fulfilled life that you can start to apply towards your life. I hope you enjoy the book, the journaling exercises offered, and I hope you enjoy the positive impact that is ignited and created from reading this book for the rest of your life!

INTRODUCTION

Is this you? You feel stuck. You feel stuck in this rinse, wash and repeat cycle that you feel trapped in. Perhaps you've found yourself coming back to your mirror in the morning again only to wonder, *is this really all there's to life?* You realize you haven't been feeling deeply fulfilled lately from the life you've created. From the outside, you may have a perfectly "normal" life with enough to be satisfied about. Many would probably even think you're fairly successful and happy. They don't actually even understand when you try to explain how unfulfilled you feel and why this is even a problem for you. But deep down, only you know some things got to change because simply put, you are not happy. And you want to be. You want more from life. You've known this for some time now, actually. You feel like you're not even scratching the surface of maximizing your potential. But you don't even know where to start.

Do you ever feel like you would do anything to live a life where you can look yourself in the mirror and say, I know who I am and I love who I am? Do you ever wish you could feel genuinely happy and in love with life? Do you miss feeling confident and excited? Do you wish that you had the skills to influence and lead yourself and others more powerfully? Do you ever feel like you are floating through life meaninglessly sometimes, and wondering when, and if, you will ever find your true purpose? Do you find yourself being so busy, yet feeling like you're not sure if you're actually growing as a soul and a human being? Do you ever wonder if you will ever be at true peace? Well, I am so glad that you're here and you are reading this right now because the Universe brought you here to help you answer some of those questions. You are exactly where you are supposed to be, as always. The Universe loves you and supports you at all times.

And by the way, I get it. These thoughts and stories I am describing were my own thoughts and stories some time ago. For me, my story unfolded something like this. I went to college, like everyone around me seemed to. I went and searched for a job because I felt I had to. Then I got a corporate job because that's what I thought everyone was doing. I had a pretty good salary so I thought it would make me happy. They (whoever "they" were now I question) said having a corporate job was perfect for a "people person" like me. So I did what I was *programmed* to do. I went to college, and I got a job. And it wasn't so bad for a little while to be honest. But then I would get bored or complacent a year or two after. And this would frustrate me. *I am making good money, so what else can I want?* So then I would get another job. Then I would get bored again. Then so naturally, I'd get another job. Then another. Over time, I started to feel empty and hopeless. Over time, I started to feel chained by my "good" salary, not inspired by it. No one around me seemed to be interested in talking about anything outside of drinking or TV shows. No one seemed to be passionate about discovering soul-level purpose, having an impact in the world, thinking about the bigger picture, and living a deeply fulfilling life. I constantly asked myself, *is it possible that maybe I can do something bigger and more meaningful with my life and career? Is there a different way of life outside of this never-ending cycle that I feel stuck in?*

My life had become so predictable and boring. I wasn't growing as a person or in my career. Then after a while, I started to realize something confronting for my ego: maybe it is not the jobs or my external circumstances to blame. I started to think, well, maybe it is *me*. Maybe it's *me* who needs to be proactive about creating the life that I love. Maybe *I* need to know what I want and just create it. In fact, no one *made* me live this life in the way I was living it. My deep yearning was that I wanted to leave a legacy in this world and make a positive impact in the world, but I didn't know what that would look like or where to even start. But I knew figuring this out would be the key to help me create my inner peace, feel deep fulfillment in my heart and freedom on a soul level that I truly desired. I knew figuring this out would help me create my own happiness. While this all started to become clear, as I started to do some serious self-reflection, I was still stuck with a giant question: *so where do I go from here?*

In this book, I will share what I learned from feeling stuck like this, and how I self-led myself towards a life that became exciting to live. I also have weaved in some stories of other amazing humans that will leave your soul on fire with inspiration. This book echoes Alfred D. Souza's philosophy, and many other spiritual leaders of the world, who says *"Happiness is a journey, not a destination. There is no way to happiness. Happiness is the way."* And here in this book, the journey is specified as the very journey from where you are, and to the destination, which is the best version of yourself. My main idea I want to get across here is that happiness can be accessed at any point during that journey towards your best self, if you consciously choose to. Choosing happiness each moment will allow you to live as the creator that you are and in an abundant state. You are a miracle on a mission to experience the blessings, the joy, the lessons and the happiness that this life has to offer for you. There are infinite possible ways to create the adventures in this journey toward your best self.

And this process of remembering who you really are, the creator that you are, will require that you actively participate in the transformation that you seek and that you are committed to *doing the inner work*. And this is where this book offers you the tools for this inner work to take place.

In this book, some topics that are covered include:

- How you get to free yourself by shedding all the heavy layers you've been wearing that used to drag you down and used to leave you feeling heavy
- How you get to feel light again
- How you get to experiment with new perspectives with a playful child's mindset as you discover start to discover yourself again
- How you get to expand through letting go of who you used to be
- How you get to connect back to who you really are and others around you

As I started to create and live a life creating the reality that I want, I started to stand in my power, remembering that I am a powerful, resilient, and infinitely creative being. My gift in this book for you is that you feel this way as well in the process of reading this. My gift in this book is the permission slip for you to access your own courage to try on different possibilities and perspectives that you've never imagined or experienced before. Through this process, you may discover that you're an artist, like I did, or that you're a writer, like I did, or that you're a speaker, like I did, or that you're an entrepreneur, like I did, that you're meant to help people as a teacher and a coach, like I did, or simply that you're limitless and that you can create whatever reality that you want in this life, like I did. And you can get excited about life again, like I did. Reading this book, you too, will get a chance to ignite your own spark of inspiration. You will have the chance to access and renew your hopes and dreams again. And you, too, get to start to create your own, most awesome story of your life and everlasting inner peace in this journey, if you choose to. I am honored that you decide to read this book and continue this journey of your self-discovery.

With gratitude,

Yuri Choi

Part I

ACCESSING THE CREATOR WITHIN YOU

CHAPTER 1

REALIZING YOU ARE A CREATOR

"Do you believe
in magic?" he asked
without a pause.
Looking into his eyes,
she said,
"I am magic."
— y.c.

You had a one-in-400 trillion chances of being conceived, but here you are. Have you ever wondered how amazing it truly is that you're alive right now? Do you know that your existence is a miracle? Let me remind you what happened from there. You were *inside* another human's womb for nine months where you magically grew a heart, hands, feet, brain, mouth, and eyes, from essentially nothing. Then, you decided it was time to be born so you detached from the womb you called home for all those months. You just innately knew, even though you didn't know how to walk, talk, run, or anything yet—you *just* knew when it was time to come out to the world and started breathing. Don't you see? You are a miracle.

The Big Bang of The Cosmic Creator

So you started breathing. You didn't have to learn how to breathe, how to make your heart beat, or how to move your little toes and fingers.

You didn't have to learn how to open your eyes or close them again to sleep. You didn't have to learn how to cry when you are hungry. You just knew how to do all of that. Without having to think about it, effortlessly, you just started being this creature called human on Earth. Then you started growing. You started translating food into fuel for your body, then you used that energy and substance to grow your bones, skin, brain, hair, and your form. You started to learn how to connect your brain as your control center for your body, and you started to move your arms, head, and legs in the way that you desired instantaneously. This desire was so natural and effortless to you.

And so you started creating. You were a creator before you knew it. You started creating new movements with your body, creating new neurons as you learned new skills in your brain. You started creating new moments and experiences within your surroundings, new relationships with your parents, friends, and family. You started creating thoughts, words, and creative drawings that would end up on your parents' fridge. Every day, you are alive, and you are creating new everything—new decisions, new memories, new experiences, and new lessons.

Don't you see? You started as a little dot. Then a miracle happened. You happened. Then BOOM, you became this human being, a magical, creative creature who can never be replicated ever again, with unique experiences to be lived and emotions to be felt and expressed. You instinctively started to radiate with so much potential and love.

It was as if it was the big bang of *your* existence, like how some people hypothesize the Universe was created. Don't you see? You are miraculous, magical, and creative. With that big bang of your existence, you created *your* Universe. And you created this reality, *your* reality. You have always been a creator, and a creator of your own reality. You *are* the ultimate cosmic creator of *your* reality.

Nothing is Created At Random

Before 1,000 BC, it wasn't really documented that anyone thought the stars and moon had any cosmic patterns. Today, we know that the stars and moons organize themselves in highly intelligent, orderly manners. The moon orbits the Earth every 27.322 days. The Earth rotates around the Sun in approximately 365 days tilted at about 23.5 degrees. This is how we have days and nights, weeks and months, and years and seasons. We've barely scratched the iceberg in understanding just how powerfully divine and highly intelligent the Universe is. Before we found any patterns to how the moon, stars, and planets are organized, we didn't know that the Universe was already working in such miraculous, systematic ways. So my question for you is this. Just because we don't have all the scientific answers for the divine order behind why your existence and my existence came about, is it a possibility that we are already divinely ordered miracles that are meant to exist in this way right now? How could you possibly think you aren't the direct consequence of millions of miracles cosmically organized and orchestrated by the Universe also? How could you possibly not believe that your existence, and your path that led you to exactly where you are, in front of this book, however you landed here, is also another divinely organized moment?

And so here you are, and you are about to get some of the questions that have been lingering on your mind answered. Here you are; and you are about to have some moments of subtle, and perhaps big, shifts that you may not have been expecting. Here you are, about to start accessing answers from within for the questions that you've been silently (or maybe loudly) asking. The truth is, the moment I started writing this book, it was all written for you. That's how the Universe works; it conspires for you. And if you stay open and receptive, you will receive whatever messages that you needed to pick up from this book in this chapter of your life to support you and your path. Everything in the Universe is being created for you. I invite you to take a deep breath, and notice what it feels like to open your heart and your mind. Notice the ease and relaxation that comes into your body when you do that. Now from that space, feel free to receive whatever lands for you from this book here and now, as a divine breadcrumb to help you get on or continue your path to create your own happiness, inner peace and success in your own life.

Declaration to the Universe: Remembering Who You Really Are

Before we go on this journey together, take a moment here to make these statements come alive for you by writing these statements here and reading them out loud in this moment. These statements serve as reminders of who you really are and to empower you and lift your spirit up for the rest of our journey together here:

I am a creator.

Write it out here: ______________________________

I was born already perfect, whole, and beautiful, and I still am.

Write it out here: ______________________________

I am a miracle.

Write it out here: ______________________________

I am a powerful creator of my own life.

Write it out here: ______________________________

Awesome. Feeling good yet? Welcome to this book! I am so glad we've completed the most important part of this whole journey—starting to remember who you really are. You are a creator with infinite possibilities. You are a creator ready to create your own happiness in your world if you choose to. With these newly ignited thoughts in mind, try these exercises below.

Journaling Exercise: Remembering your Miraculous Moments

For a moment, I invite you to focus your attention to the blessings and miracles that have already manifested. Take a moment to reflect on your own life and find examples that support that you have already been experiencing miracles in your own life.

Here are some examples I've heard from other people.

- Maybe your mother and father only met once on a plane before they fell in love, which led to your existence.

- Maybe you had a life-threatening situation you should not have survived, but not only did you live through it, but it changed your life for the better.
- Maybe you dreamt about going to a concert forever, and one day you were presented with a ticket for it and your dreams came true.
- Maybe you thought you were not flexible growing up, but you can now do yoga and handstands and have realized your body's new capabilities.
- Maybe the exact time you needed a mentor in your life, someone showed up, became your guardian angel, and led you to the next chapter in your life.

Here's my list as an example:

1. When I was 3 months old, I got really sick. My parents invited the Catholic priest to the ICU to give me a prayer for the dying, because they weren't sure I was going to make it. However, I survived and became healthy! (Ta-da!)
2. When I was five, a tall piece of furniture tripped and fell on my left leg and broke it. If it had landed anywhere else, I would not be alive!
3. When I was in a bad car accident in 2008, but I walked away with only a little cut on my face. That car accident is what led me to yoga, which is now one of my biggest blessings and passions.

4. When I was young, I used to dream I was talking to angels. We would have conversations about life.
5. I once saw a giant butterfly, bigger than my face, when I was in the magical Bali. Every time I see a butterfly, it is a spiritual sign for me that reminds me of my dad who has passed on. Later that day, I realized it was Father's Day in Bali!

...and so on.... Now it's your turn. What miracles have you been blessed with that serve as *reminders* that you are and can acknowledge that miracles are present in your life?

List your five miracle stories here:

1. ____

2. ____

3. ____

4. ____

5. ____

____

____

Are you starting to remember some stories reminding you of all the amazing moments in your life yet? This book will guide you toward your journey in *remembering* that you are a miraculous creature who can find and create your own joy and happiness in your heart at all times.

Remember, you can choose to feel like that baby being born and re-creating your reality at any time. You can start with a blank slate whenever you want! You can start over anytime. You can start over and start creating your life *now*! So now that we've come to an agreement that you're a miracle and that you get to create the life you truly want, let's talk about creating your own happiness and get started by defining the concept of happiness together in the next chapter.

CHAPTER 2

CREATING YOUR OWN DEFINITION OF HAPPINESS

True happiness is subtle.
It's not something that hits
you with a high, or has peaks
and valleys, it just is.
True contentment is modest.
It does not need to boast because
the positive aura naturally
radiating fills any room
without effort.
True joy is being present.
no accumulation of joyful moments
of the past or anticipated fortune
of the future will make you happy
this very moment.
So smile right now,
love steadily
and carry on your grateful days
effortlessly;
And there you will be
just as you are,
Happy.
— y.c.

How do you define joy, happiness, or fulfillment? Are you happy right now? How do you know? Where do you feel it in your body when you know you are happy? Do money, cars, homes, new clothes *make* you happy? Do you feel happy when you are drunk or high? Does laughter equal happiness? What "makes" you happy anyway? Would you be open to you trying on the idea that you can be happy anytime you choose to, regardless of external factors?

How Our Generation Thinks About Life and Happiness

How do our millennials think about happiness? A study found that millennials value "getting rich" as one of the most important goals in life. In the same survey, millennials indicated that the second-most important goal in life is "to be famous." Millennials are also more depressed than past generations.

In fact, depression is rampant in America across all generations. Did you know that 129 suicides happen in America every day on average? That's 47,085 per year. Since 1990, antidepressant prescription has increased by 400 percent.

And that these tragedies happen even among rich, famous, and seemingly happy celebrities continues to surprise us: Robin Williams, Kate Spade, Heath Ledger, Avicci. What was possibly missing for them, when they seemed to have it all?

Happiness Later, But What About Happiness Now?

Thinking being rich or famous will bring happiness poses a fundamental problem for most: we believe happiness belongs in the future or externally, not in our present moment.

No matter where you are in your timeline of life, you will

one day decide consciously, "Okay, right now I am happy" for you *to ever* be happy. And if you don't have the skill to access that "Okay, right now I am happy" feeling now, you won't know how to access it all of the sudden when you reach a certain "milestone," whether it be how much money you have or the number of houses you own.

How often do we hear people (or ourselves) say, "I would be happy if I had ______________________________?"

- I'd be happy if I just had a boyfriend or girlfriend.
- I'd be happy if I just would get married.
- I'd be happy if I had five million dollars in the bank.
- I'd be happy if I just had this promotion.
- I'd be happy if I just went on this trip.
- I'd be happy if I started my own business.

Be, Do, Have

So this is how most people think:

When I **HAVE** that car,

I'll **DO** the things successful and happy people do,

So I can **BE** happy.

But what happens when you get that car, and you still don't know how to be happy because you never practiced being happy *now*?

Okay, so then this is how it goes. Well I have this car, but I am still not happy… (I don't know how to surrender to being happy).

BUT,

When I **HAVE** that house,

I'll finally **DO** the things successful and happy people do,

So I can **BE** happy!

Then what happens when you have the house?

Okay, well I have the dream house, but I am still not happy…

Okay, okay,

When I **HAVE** a baby and a wife,

I'll finally **DO** the things successful and happy people do,

So I can **BE** happy.

And so on. So you get the point.

To be happy now, I invite you to…flip the script. Commit to being happy *now* so you can do the things happy people do, so you can have the things that happy people have.

To expand: **Be** happy now, knowing you can create an emotional state you want at any time. Remember you are a powerful creator who has the infinite potential to create anything you want, including your own emotions. If you can create any emotional state in the world for yourself, you wouldn't create an emotion like fear, anxiety, or negative emotions, would you? So any time you are in a negative emotion, or any emotions that don't serve you, remember you are *choosing* not to be creative. You are living in the past, and not in the moment. Recognizing this, you can choose to be creative and craft the emotion you want to access from within *right now.* Throughout this book, many exercises will be offered to help you access the skills and knowledge to practice being happy right *now.*

You Can Choose How You Feel Now

Have you ever seen someone who was in a heated argument, then go to work and put on their work face and moved on with their day, as if nothing happened? You can choose the emotional state you want to align with at any time. Dr. Joe Dispenza, an expert on linking spirituality and neuroscience around the concept of creating your own reality, says "Your personality creates your personal reality. Your personality is made up of how you act, how you think and how you feel."

When someone has a positive, happy personality, would you agree that more connections, friends, and opportunities usually present themselves to these people? Knowing we can create any emotional state we desire, we can commit to choosing a life filled with happiness, joy and inner peace, at any time.

Defining Happiness

And this book is really the journey of finding out how to close that gap between where you are, and where you think "happiness" is. The more and more we close that gap, we recognize that really, any moment can offer joy, peace and fulfillment. In this book, being powerfully tapped into each present moment and finding lessons on the journey of going from where you are now, to your "destination" which is your best self, is defined as happiness. Happiness is not something that is "achieved" just at the end of that destination but during the entire journey of it. Happiness is a choice at any given time and can be accessed when we set an intention and surrender into it, moment by moment. Happiness is the process and the very journey of becoming your best self. And that best self is the version of you who takes the power back as a creator that you've always been. That path and each person's version of "best-self" and what it looks like to create your life will look different for every single human. There's no right, wrong, better or worse here of how we envision that best version of ourselves. My request for you though, is that you create your own meaning of happiness, and not take on someone else's meaning that you've subconsciously taken on throughout your life. Earlier, we discovered that millennials think what they think makes them happy is being rich and famous. These ideals of happiness are ideals that were adopted from the media or culture. It's time to take the power back and define your own ideals of your best self and your own definition of happiness and success. A part of that will come from taking the time to reflect and learn about yourself, as well as creating a vision for what your best self looks like. This book will help you through that process.

Journaling Exercise

1. What does happiness mean to you? What do you think of when you hear the word *happiness?*

____

____

____

2. Who taught you that? What influences have helped you shape this meaning for you? (think about the influences in your life that shaped

your definition of happiness, such as parents, family, culture, social circles, school, religion, sports, etc.)

____

____

____

3. What are some things you "have" in your life that you thought would make you happy, (but as soon as you got to "have" them, you decided you needed more things to be happy)?

____

____

____

CHAPTER 3

CREATING AN UNAPOLOGETIC LIFE TO BE HAPPY

Take the courage
to be the one who rebels
from the predetermined trends
of the crowd;
to be the one who celebrates
being anything but
being labeled as "normal;"
to be the one who confidently
denies the expectations set
by anyone other than oneself.
Then with a hint of a smile on your face,
and a whiff of passionate laughter
on your breath,
be unapologetically
you.
— y.c.

My Story of Dimming My Own Light

In 2009, I was valedictorian of my class at Chapman University. I graduated with two degrees in four years: a B.A. in Psychology and a B.S. in Business Marketing. I got mostly all A's in all my classes, except one. I never posted one photo of me giving a speech at my college graduation. I tried not to let any photos leak out of me holding my valedictorian trophy. I never mentioned it to anyone for many years, although some people found out through my close friends. I hid behind words like "modest" and "humble," but the truth was, deep down, I didn't feel I was worthy of it and cringed whenever the subject came up.

In my mind, getting two degrees in four years, and taking a maximum number of credits every semester, every summer and winter break, still wasn't enough. Spending ten-plus hours a day, and most of my Saturdays and Sundays in the library before going to parties while everyone else was relaxing, hanging out, and beaching it...still didn't feel like enough. Being part of the executive board for the biggest honor society on campus, while being in two other honor societies wasn't enough. Always having two part-time jobs for four years wasn't enough. And somehow managing to party six nights out of seven days—that was really all I ever talked about on social media and to friends.... Of all the things I was accomplishing, *that* was what I was proud of back then. People thought I was a party girl and social butterfly. I wanted to fit in, so I thought being a hardworking, nerdy, 4.0 student made me stand out in a way I didn't want to. It didn't feel cool. I was stuck in this destination disease—that my worth, my happiness, was somewhere when I achieved more. Those things were anywhere, but here and now. So, no matter what I achieved, I didn't feel I was enough.

Words I Took to Heart from My Mom

When I moved to the United States, my mom never let me forget: "Yuri, you are a minority in this country. You have to work 200 percent harder than most people to have what others who grew up here have. Always remember that." While this served me because it pushed me and caused me to create an unusual level of resilience, it also wired me to think I always had to work 200 percent harder to be as worthy as others. I got two degrees while others got one. I worked out twice a day while others went to the gym once. I partied twice as hard. I drank twice as much. I studied twice as hard. I had two part-time jobs. So deep down, I was still overcompensating for my wounds from when I first moved to the U.S. What most people didn't know was my valedictorian trophy was a form of revenge, not inspiration. That's why I didn't feel proud of it. It was the hardworking evidence of me, in my mind, barely exceeding the survival zone, and really, moving away from the pain of my limiting belief that I was not equal to others unless I worked harder. So when I held that trophy in my hand on my graduation day, I didn't feel that good. Secretly, I was exhausted, and I asked myself, "How much longer and harder will I have to work like this to keep up just being equal to everyone else?"

Time Hop Back to 1998

One of my teachers cried when my mom and I told her I was immigrating to the U.S. My mom and I were moving to Denver so my mom could marry my future stepdad and we could start a new life and family together. My fifth-grade teacher and the dean told my mom, "Losing Yuri to America is like losing a national treasure." Even at a young age, I cared deeply about people, gave my best to everything, and showed up with integrity. I had amazing support, respect, and love from my teachers and classmates. I had amazing, authentic friendships with every single one of my classmates. I was class president, had many friends, and won all sorts of awards in Korea—from academic to artistic and athletic. I won the "model student" award many times. In a folder somewhere, I have twenty-eight awards I won in my first five years of grade school in Korea. (They're a little award happy there.)

But when I moved here at age eleven, overnight, I became a nobody, a loser, an ESL student no one could understand.

I couldn't speak English, let alone understand my homework.

I once misunderstood my homework, thinking we had to write a three-page essay when all we had to do was write down three words. I spent seven hours doing that assignment, while everyone else did it in a few seconds. I felt like I was deaf, mute, and culturally inept because of my language barrier. And I told myself I did "stupid" things because of it.

People sometimes said awful things about me and other ESL students right in front of us because they thought we couldn't understand them. But I could. I could understand them. I just couldn't speak fluently and confidently yet. And I understood their energy even if I didn't understand everything they were saying. Meanwhile, I was going through puberty and adjusting to my changing body. I was also adjusting to a new family life. At home, I had a new father, and a new family dynamic. My parents were both working very hard to start their own bakery, so they couldn't spend much time with me. They worked tirelessly, fourteen-plus hours a day, seven days a week. That meant I had to figure things out for myself.

Winning as Revenge

One day, during my second month in the U.S., I was in the girls bathroom. Someone had made a mess in one of the stalls and left it. It was *really* gross. Then these two pretty American girls walked in. They opened the door to the stall and exclaimed, "Eww! That's disgusting! It was probably one of those retarded ESL kids." I was an ESL kid. And I was smart. But they thought I was "retarded." That made me really angry. Instantly, school became about me vs. them, and proving my worth to them, whoever *they* were.

Are You Moving Away From Fear or Moving Toward an Inspiration?

Today, I teach my clients that anger is an action-activating emotion. It is a survival emotion that when activated in the body allows you to have massive focus. My anger pushed me to take massive action to move away from pain. And I did take massive action that first summer! I was determined to prove those girls—and everyone—wrong. From that day, my achievement equaled revenge. I was no longer creating, working hard, and making friends out of joy and love like I did in Korea. I read thirty books that first month (The Baby-Sitters Club series and a few others, and it took *forever* to read all of them.) I wrote down every word I didn't know and its definition in my notebook. Mind you, I had no computer back then, so I had to use the manual dictionary to learn each word.

I was determined. The next fall, I marched into my counselor's office and said, "I am ready to be in a regular English class."

"Your English sounds better," she replied, "but no one ever leaves ESL after their first semester here."

"I am ready. I read thirty books this summer. Please give me a test or something."

"I mean, I can give you a test, but it most likely will be another year or two before you test out of ESL."

"I am ready; please let me take the test," I repeated, unwilling to give up.

That semester, I was proudly placed in a regular English class with those girls from the bathroom who had made fun of me. The following year, I was in an Advanced English class. By high school, I was in the college level English classes.

Winning, But Still Not Feeling Good

Yes, I am proud of how well I learned English. However, during my teenage years, I always felt like I had to do more to fit in. Deep down, I was still that really hurt eleven-year-old, who didn't fit in in any way. I felt like I always had to prove my worth, just in case someone questioned it. Deep down, I didn't feel like I was enough. So it is no surprise that without healing those wounds or doing the inner work, even as a college valedictorian, I still felt I wasn't enough. All those years, my desire to "fit in" and to be liked was bigger than standing proudly in my light.

Today After Doing the Inner Work

Since then, I've done a lot of self-study, inner work, growing, and owning my worth.

In early 2019, I won the Achievement Award at the Legends Tour Habitude Warrior Conference. The plaque reads "Presented to: Yuri Choi - For your ongoing perseverance." At the conference, I was on the same stage as legends and global leaders in the self-help world, Brian Tracy, Dan Clark, Loral Langemeier and Sharon Lechter. I had no idea the founder of the conference and the *Habitude Warrior* team would surprise me with it. I burst into tears. This award felt different. I wasn't trying to prove my worth. I was just being myself, and they saw something special in me, and in my character. *That* meant a lot. This award wasn't about meeting or exceeding anyone else's expectations or standards or trying to prove anything. It was about *me* standing in my own bright light, doing what I love, serving and inspiring people out of passion. I was finally back to my old real self, the one that would create out of pure joy, love, and passion.

A faint inner voice still wants to say something like, "But, Yuri, do you really deserve this? Who are you to share your wins when so many amazing people are in this world? Don't you feel like you're bragging about something you don't deserve?

So by telling you about it, I am sharing while putting down my mask of being humble and standing in my worth, truth, and joy.

This is about owning both my darkest shadows and my brightest light, because both ends of those spectrums make me who I am. It is also me putting my fear aside and being courageous. I know deep down that my truest intention is to inspire you with everything I vulnerably share about myself.

And that means the world to me—because I feel truly seen for who I really am.

"Being unapologetic means that I will be all of me. I will no longer shrink or compromise myself by playing small so others will not feel insecure in my presence."

- Lisa Nichols

Unapologetically Own Who You Are

My intention to share this with you is because: I want you to own your wins. I want you to own your failures. I want you to own your light. And I want you to own your shadows. I want you to own, love, appreciate, accept all of you without judgement. I want to remind you that you get to give yourself permission to shine in your brightest light and shine in your biggest failures. Never dim your light to "fit in" or help others feel more comfortable, especially if your deepest wish is to reach your full potential, be fulfilled, and be happy. Because those things are exactly what you will sacrifice on the way. We, the Universe and everyone in it, *want* to see your light. We are excited and ready to be inspired by your light. So thank you for shining bright. I hope you start right now, if you haven't already. Let's make this world a brighter place together.

Journaling Exercise

1. What are some of your biggest wins that you don't share with people often enough because you're scared they might judge you?

___

___

2. If you were to share those wins, who could be inspired by them?

CHAPTER 4

ACCESSING CLARITY

You are what you eat.
You are what you do.
You are what you think.

Eat only what makes you
proud daily,
your day meaningful,
your efforts productive, and
your exertion of energy
positively impactful to others.

Think only what makes you
free and your heart light,
identify your darkest fears,
and constantly color them with hopes,
and create your castle of your dreams.
because there will be a time...

When your bones will be so strong
they keep your hopes up,
your energy will be so positive
it keeps your heart steady,
and your hopes will be so meaningful
you color life onto others,

then there will be times when you get caught up in your creation, your existence, who you are, and what you are made of. It becomes so complex you forget, oh you forget, what makes your castle, what is important, why dream, fears—oh I fear, no, no, no, no. Stop.

Take a deep breath and just focus.

It's simple.
I am what I eat,
I am what I do,
I am what I think.
— y.c.

Clarity Is Power

"How did I end up here?"

"What is really going on?"

When my clients first come to me, they usually feel a sense of panic, an emptiness, a feeling of being unfulfilled, or dread about the lives or habits they feel stuck in. And the first thing I inspire them to create with me is clarity.

Dan Clark, an international speaker, and one of the main contributors to the Chicken Soup for the Soul series, once said this when we were in Dallas at a speakers' dinner after an event. Something he said about clarity really stuck out to me: "Even if you're calling an Uber, if you don't know where you are, and you don't know where you're going, there's nothing the Uber can do for you." That is the first thing I remind my clients when we start working together. The first step is getting clear on where they are, in all areas of their lives, as a starting point. Clarity is power.

Who Are You?

The first step in transforming yourself is becoming aware of where you currently are right now. If you could take a snapshot life right now, what would that look like?

When you go for your annual physical exam, the first thing your doctor does is take a snapshot of your body by looking at different angles of your health. They might take blood tests, listen to your heart, and check your blood pressure. They might check your weight and ask you about your diet. There's different ways to check your body's health.

It is also important to regularly take a snapshot of your life. When was the last time you did so?

Below, we'll check your pulse of your life through an exercise called the Snapshot of Your Life. I participated in this powerful exercise at an enlightening business retreat with the Greatness Foundation in Bali. It was an exercise very similar to this that invited clarity into my life. From the clarity I accessed from this exercise allowed me to get clear on where I was at the time, and this gave me an easier time accessing where I wanted to go from there as my next step into becoming the best version of myself. Ultimately, that led to me deciding to write my first book.

"Clarity of mind means clarity of passion, too."
– Blaise Pascal

Those who wish to find clarity in their purpose and their passions in life, the first step is to invite clarity into your life.

Exercise 1: Who Am I Really?

Let's start uncovering where you are by asking a very simple, yet powerful question that most people find hard to answer at a glance. The question is "Who are you?"

Fill in the blank spaces with whatever that comes up for you.

For me. I am a daughter. I am a coach. I am a speaker. I am a writer. I am a yogi. I am a soul. I am love. And so on.

How would you answer this question: Who are you?

1. I am ______________________________
2. I am ______________________________
3. I am ______________________________
4. I am ______________________________
5. I am ______________________________

Exercise 2: Snapshot of Life

If someone asked you to describe your life right now, factually without judgment or stories around it, how would you describe it? Would you be able to describe it in all the different areas of your life? Let's take a quick snapshot of your life and see what that looks like using the Snapshot of Life exercise.

It is common to feel surprised, or even a little disappointed, when you do the Snapshot of Life exercise and the below Life Review exercise.

It's like when you go to the dentist, and you haven't been flossing, so that is showing up after during checkup and may be an area of your dental health you can bring more awareness and attention to. I invite you to be present with whatever comes up for you, and I also invite you to remember that awareness is the first step in creating the best version of yourself!

Take a look at all the different areas of your life listed below. Use the questions to rate each area on a scale of 1 to 10, with 1 being *not* satisfactory and 10 being at your full maximum potential.

1. Emotional/Mental Health

- How do you feel every day emotionally and mentally? ____
- How long do you stay in negative emotions (1 being long and 10 being not long at all)? ____
- How do you feel getting up every morning? ____

2. Finances

- How clear are you about your current financial health? ____
- How do you feel when you think about money & finances? ____
- How abundant (10) or stressed (1) do you *feel* when it comes to your finances? _____

3. Physical Health

- Is your body generally pain-free and feeling good (10) rather than in pain (0) on a day-to-day basis? ____
- How energized do you feel every morning? ____

- How nourished and lively do you feel in your body? __

4. Business/Work

- How fulfilled do you feel at work or in your business? ____
- How much of your potential and strengths are being used? ____
- How successful do you feel in your work? ____

5. Family/Friends

- How connected do you feel to your friends and family? ____
- How supported do you feel amongst your family & friends? ___
- How harmonious are you with the people you spend the most time with? ___

6. Significant Other/Romance

- How happy are you with your romantic life? ___
- How does the time and attention you give your romantic life correlate with your goals in this area? (10: supports my growth) ____
- Do you feel you are the type of partner your ideal / current partner for your current or future partner? ____

7. Spirituality

- How connected do you feel to God, higher power or the Universe? ____
- Have you developed a relationship with God or the Universe? ___

- How spiritually connected do you feel on a day-to-day basis? ____

8. Lifestyle

- How satisfied or happy are you with the way you spend your free time? ____
- Do you have a lot of fun and laughter in your life? ____
- How aligned are your general eating, drinking, and substance habits with your goals and vision? ____

9. Personal Growth

- Do you do something to grow and stretch outside of your comfort zone every day? ____
- Do you spend time and resources on personal growth in the last month? ____
- Do you learn something new every day? ____

10. Creativity & Self Expression

- Do you engage in creative activities often?____
- Do you feel that you are expressing yourself authentically on a consistent basis? ____
- How self-expressed do you feel on a day-today basis? ____

Now add up each section and find an average here.

For example, for #1, if you scored 5, 7, and 6, add 5 + 7 + 6 which is 18, then divide by 3, which is 6. Then you would put "6" on the scorecard below.

1. ____ 2. ____ 3. ____ 4. ____ 5. ____

6. ____ 7. ____ 8. ____ 9. ____ 10.____

Looking at the Snapshot of Life, what areas of your life are most fulfilled? What areas do you get to work on and pour love and attention on?

Great. How did that feel? Do you feel more clarity?

Now that you know where your life is today, I invite you to appreciate what this exercise revealed to you with love, compassion, and no judgment. This exercise may bring up some powerful emotions—it did for me the first time I did it.

Now take a good objective look at the person you have been.

This is who you were a moment ago. If you choose, you can continue to be this person, but you've picked up this book because you want to live a happier life. I am offering you the reminder that you have an opportunity to return to a blank slate. You no longer have to be the person you have been. If you were free to create your best self, without justifying your past, as if you were a baby being nurtured in a womb again, who would you create? What if I told you that from this point on, nothing that has happened matters? Can you give yourself permission to break up with your old self so you can create your new self from scratch? So you can let go of all your fears, stories, and limiting beliefs that once held you back?

The stories that hold you back might look something like: "Well, I went to college and I told my parents I'd be a doctor, so I can't become an artist—that would disappoint my parents and myself!" or "I got my master's degree to become a teacher, so I can't travel the world and have other jobs! I have a job that pays my bills so I can't leave that job!" All of those stories—are you ready to let them go?

Now that you've let go of who you have been, you are ready to create who you are becoming, with this moment as your starting point.

"If you hear a voice within you say 'you cannot paint,'
then by all means paint, and that voice will be silenced."

-Vincent Van Gogh

Journaling Exercise

1. What did you learn about yourself from the *Snapshot of Life exercise?*

____

____

____

2. What are you most proud of in your life?

____

____

____

3. What has been your biggest challenge?

____

____

____

4. What areas of your life do you want to change or improve? Why?

CHAPTER 5

CREATING YOUR BEST SELF AVATAR

She could not see
the magic
she was creating within her,
just yet.
— y.c.

Now that we are clear on where you currently are, you might be wondering, "*Where are we headed from here?*" The answer: to the best version of yourself!

Accessing your massively creative mind, imagine that your life is a giant white canvas upon which to create your most Divine Self. This is the person you were always meant to be. This is the person who shows up when you open your heart and soul to the infinite possibilities of the Universe.

Two questions can help you access this vision:

1. If you won $333 million in the lottery and never had to work another day for money, what would you do with your money that is meaningful?
2. If you knew you had three months to live, what would you start doing today?

When money becomes a non-limiting factor and time becomes a limiting factor, you can find out what their heart truly desires. I am curious about you now. What did you answer to those two questions above? If you truly can give yourself full permission to be whoever you want to be without any fears, who would you be? What kinds of relationships would you cultivate with the people in your life? What would you do with that money? What would you want your legacy to be? How would you want people in the world to remember you? How would you want the closest people in your life to remember you?

This is the version of yourself who lives from your purpose and led by the passion of your heart. The version of yourself that reveals what you truly care about in the world.

So now imagine this... If I told you that you can architect the persona of this best version of yourself anyway, what would become possible for you? What would a version of yourself be like that is doing 9 or 10 out of 10 in those ten areas of your life as revealed in the Snapshot of Life exercise? How would you feel that in your body? How would you talk, walk, and act? Where would you go? What would you do? How would you interact with the world? Tap into the emotional state of already being this person you created in your mind, and really envision what it would be like to *be* that version of yourself.

Your Best Self Avatar Creation:

Let's name this best version of yourself __________ (your name).

What traits makes this avatar the best version of you? Describe them in detail here. What would this person be like? (At the end of this chapter, you will have an opportunity to get more detailed with this avatar. For now, journal whatever comes up for you.)

____

____

____

____

____

Practice Accessing Your Best Self

When Beyoncé came out with her album, *I Am Sasha Fierce* (2008), she said she wanted to break free from her past persona of being innocent and professional, to a sexier, more liberal, and experimental persona that allowed her to step into a different version of herself. This process is not necessarily the same as "Fake it 'til you make it." This is you calling in your future self and actually being it for a few seconds, as you name this persona and visualize him or her. Then over time, the few seconds become a few minutes, then a few hours, and then a few days, and over time, you can step into that version of yourself 24 hours a day, everyday.

You get to practice accessing this version of yourself more and more. You can do this by imagining that you are inviting every cell and part of your body to experience what it would feel like to be that version of yourself. Stay there for a moment. What does life look and feel like from being that version of yourself? How would you treat others? How would you carry yourself? How would you carry on conversations? How would you interact with the world? Would you dress differently? Would you eat different kinds of food? As you start to visualize a day being this version of yourself, you're calling in the reality that your future self would be experiencing, now. You are closing the gap between the future and now. Overtime, your reality starts to catch up. When you start living from the vibration of your best self, and your mind and body are truly congruent, you have the power to tap into that reality, now. You are essentially signaling to the Universe that you're ready for that desired reality. The Universe will start gladly reorganizing the world around you to help you create your desired reality because you are already being that version of yourself. Yes, the Universe creates the reality that matches the frequency that you are *being*, so it's important to not only create this avatar, but also practice being that version of you as often as possible. The Universe will gladly catch up to you, when you're living as if you are that version of yourself.

Creating this avatar of your best self, you are essentially planting a seed into the future where infinite possibilities are available. By practicing and continually aligning to this avatar's being, you are watering this seed so that this version of yourself can grow. Through meditations, developing self-leadership, getting clear on your values, tuning into the frequency of your most creative and abundant mindset, and turning on your faith, you can access this version of yourself even faster.

You can also start having a conversation with that best version of you. When you can access the wisdom from your future self, it is powerful because you can start to source your best advice from within. So open up your heart to see what your future self would share with you, so you can become that person. You can follow the meditation example below to do this, if you wish.

Meditation

Sit on a comfortable pillow or blanket. Close your eyes. Take a deep breath through your nose. Exhale through your mouth, letting all the stale energy out. Then start your ujjayi breath by constricting the back of your throat with your mouth closed and breathing through your nose. Once you have fallen into a state of meditation, ask your best self, "Hi, my future best self. Thank you for always guiding me towards you. What is my next best step to take to become you? What is my next logical step toward my greatest potential that you have already accessed from where you are. Then, sit in your meditation and just listen. Sometimes I sit in the silence for five minutes, and sometimes for two hours. See what comes through for you. You will be surprised and delighted to discover the clarity you will gain about where you are headed. I have heard many messages this way.

How I Became a Writer

"Occupation?" it asked. On the scroll down menu, it read "writer." My heart started beating faster. Wow, could I call myself a writer for this account? Can I try on this identity? I was staring at the page finalizing creating a new username on *Instagram*. I was creating a new account just for my poetry that night, inspired by a friend. At that time, I had been writing poetry for years on my own, but when I tried to write down on my new Instagram account that I was going to call myself a *writer*, it felt scary. I felt like if someone were to find out this is me, they would laugh at me. Typing out that I was actually a writer and a poet seemed weird. Who was I to call myself that? What will people think when they find out I am just a person who writes blogs and poetry for fun? All these irrational fears started consuming my mind. Yes, all over one little question on my Instagram profile page. That is what our ego does when we try to shift to a different identity of any sort, even if it is towards our purpose or our best self. Our ego only likes what's familiar and comfortable. Deep down though, our souls know when a connection exists to something that seems aligned. And my soul in that moment was so excited. I heard myself somewhere deep in my heart, "Wow, I get to be a writer!" It felt like an intuitive whisper from my soul, letting me know this is my divine breadcrumb to follow towards my best self.

At the time, I was working as a corporate sales associate for years. My friend, who was helping me create the account, reminded me I am, indeed, a writer—after all! He reminded me that the world was ready to hear my poetry and my writing. "If this helps you, you are an *aspiring* writer," he said, "and that is enough for you to put down your occupation as 'writer.' Plus, it's just Instagram." He was unaware of my internal battle with my ego, which was trying so hard to keep my old identity alive, unwilling to be flexible for new possibilities and new identities. I looked at him blankly. I had already been in corporate sales for ten years, so what could I possibly aspire to be now? Would I ever be able to actually become a writer? It sounds weird that this was even my doubt now that I am thinking back, but I thought I was too "old" to try on a different career path. Who am I to dream about being a writer and being an *official* poet? I'm already stuck in this path of being in corporate forever. I work, then I work for a few more decades, then I retire. I was told to climb the corporate ladder. That's what I do right? Work hard at one path forever, right?

Despite this internal ego struggle, I decided to try it out. "I know. I know, ego," I told my ego. "It doesn't make sense, but I am going to try it out." So underneath my account name on my Instagram profile, I chose my occupation as "Writer/Poet." It felt weird. It didn't feel 100 percent right because I didn't *feel* like a writer yet. I was just a person who had written lots of blog posts and countless poems and just really enjoyed writing. Did I *deserve* to call myself a writer yet? I didn't even know about Laws of Attraction principles at the time, and my logical mind didn't really believe it was possible yet. But I decided it was worth a try. Why not? And my friend was right. It's *just* Instagram. Why not be playful about it? I decided to go against the resistance I felt from my mean inner critic that said, "No, no, you are lying; you aren't a writer yet." I decided to listen to the part of me that was saying intuitively, "Yes, yes, you are. You were born to be a writer, and you will become this new identity, sooner than later." And for a moment, I accessed my future self. I actually believed it for a second, and I felt in my body what it would be like to be a writer and publish a book or poetry series one day. So the seed was planted in the Universe. And here I am writing this book many years later, because of that small but monumental moment of planting a new possibility in my mind field.

Planting the Thought Seed

That was a powerful moment for me; it was the first time I let my mind believe for half a second that my new identity as a writer and poet was even possible. I had planted the seed in my own mind and could now start growing the trees of possibilities in my garden of limitless potential. Because I planted the seed then, even though it was uncomfortable, I am now writing this book. Think about what you can plant the seed of becoming today. We will explore this topic more in the Expression section, but for now, write it out, tell people, do whatever you have to do to let the Universe know you are serious about planting this seed and starting the process of creating a new identity. Even if it initially feels weird because your ego doesn't really like change, just plant the seed in your head that it is a possibility. Sometimes, that seed is all it takes for the idea to blossom. In time, watered with divine guidance, timing and many small to big actions towards this dream that naturally start to unfold, it will come true. Slowly, I started to feel more comfortable sharing my writings, poems, and thoughts with other people because of the simple act of starting and posting my most vulnerable writing to the world through that *Instagram* account. Because of the positive feedback and increase in the number of followers who loved my work, I started to write more. I became bolder about showing up authentically when I would write, and with the content I would share. And over time, I have gotten to the point where I can say I am not only a writer, but an author. So start today. Think about who you want to become, and start acting and living from that identity, whatever that looks like to you. You are powerful. Your best version of yourself is waiting for you in the future.

Exercise

Create the avatar of your best self:

1. What was the name you gave yourself for this avatar of yours?

____

____

2. What adjectives would you use to describe the best version of yourself?

____

3. What does this version of you do that you're currently not doing?

4. How does your best self treat others?

5. What would he or she do each morning?

6. What would he or she focus on every day?

CHAPTER 6

SELF-LEADING YOURSELF

So hear me out
as I roar like a lion,
with a white daisy in my hair,
fearless,
all while flirting with
the world.
I'm ready to be seduced
by you and
all your magic, Universe,
but you also won't get away
without a taste
of my charm.
— y.c.

You Are the Leader, the CEO of Your Own Life

Magnificent soul, so if you could be that best version of yourself right now, what would you create in your reality today? What are you starting to see as new possibilities for yourself? What will you help you thrive as you strive towards your best version of yourself? Maybe you've always wanted to be a musician. Or maybe you've always had an idea for a brilliant new product or business. Or are you thinking about entering a bodybuilding contest? What about writing a book and becoming an author? Starting a YouTube channel? Yes, yes, yes! You are starting to access the possibilities now! And yes, those are all 100 percent possible for you!

Become the CEO of Creating Your Best Self

... But the first thing you get to know in your heart is:

"Yes, I, too, can."

Or maybe this question resonates with your soul better:

"Why not me?"

When the legendary motivational speaker Les Brown was young, he was told that he was "mentally retarded" by the school. One day, when his English teacher asked him to write something on the board, Brown answered, "No, sir, I can't because I was told I am 'retarded' and that I wouldn't be able to do that." Les Brown told him that's what his other teacher told him.

Then his English teacher said something to Les Brown that changed his life forever. "Someone's opinion of you doesn't have to become your reality." For Les Brown, that was the first time he realized he could create his life in the direction he wanted, and that he got to be the CEO of his own life, regardless of what others *told* him he needed to be. It was the moment when he realized no one can take away the power from him to declare and create who he gets to be for the world.

So how do you ignite that deep belief within you, and make that dream of yours manifest into physical reality? Answer: by becoming your own CEO, boss, and leader. Self-leadership is the driver's seat of the vehicle (your body) toward your best self.

Removing the Fun Blockers to Self-Leadership

Self-leadership is the ability to lead yourself to a goal, without yourself getting in the way of your goal. It sounds simple but how many times do we get stopped by our own fight-or-flight response (fear), our own disempowering stories, and limiting beliefs about who we are and what we can and cannot do? I call these the *fun blockers. Fun blockers are anything* that gets in the way of you living your most fun, amazing life. Because isn't it true that these fears just block the fun, joy, and playfulness out of your life? Think about that fear of people judging you. That's a fun blocker. That fear of failure? *That's* a fun blocker. Perfectionism? That's a fun blocker.

Self-leadership is activated when the mind and the body are working together, not getting stopped by these fun blockers. Think of your mind as the CEO of your body, and your body as the body of an organization that helps the vision the CEO created come to life. When the entire "organization" and the "leader" (your body and your mind respectively) work together, that's when you get to lead yourself powerfully toward your own vision and goals. Achieving self-leadership effectively can be broken down to this step-by-step process. I've broken down the steps so you can understand it better by using a metaphor of a CEO in a business or an organization:

- The CEO creates a vision so that the body of the organization, such as different teams and managers, knows what they are there to create. The CEO is a metaphor for your mind. Your mind sets forth the vision. The *vision* here is your *best self-avatar.* The body of the organization is a metaphor for your physical body. Your body is the part of you that carries out the tasks and implements the vision. Just as the CEO cannot create his vision (your b come true alone, the mind cannot create anything in the physical reality without the body. The CEO (the mind) and the body of the organization (your body) are interconnected and interdependent.

- The CEO sets forth the values and standards for the body of the organization to operate efficiently and orderly. Your mind sets forth values and rules for your body to follow. These can look like setting your core values down and ensuring that your body follows them to be a good person. This can look like creating the standards to work out every day and follow a morning routine so that your body knows what the ground rules are to stay healthy.
- The CEO hires and fires employees based on if they are on board with his vision and adheres to the values and the standards of what he sets forth. This is how she or he ensures that the organization stays aligned to the culture the CEO wishes to create. Your mind (CEO) consciously filters and hires only the "employees" that are on board. *Employees* here are the metaphor for your thoughts, that work toward that goal. Hire and pay attention only to the "employees (thoughts)" that are there to truly serve your vision. Fearlessly fire those thoughts that are not

aligned to your values or your vision. Let your fears go. Let the gossip of your inner critic go. Fire them ruthlessly.

- The CEO checks in with the body of the organization to ensure it is optimally operating to work toward the vision, to make sure that everything runs smoothly long-term. Reduced turnover rate is efficient for the health of the organization for sustained success. The CEO checks in to see, are the teams and managers happy? Are they getting what they need? Are they living a balanced life? Same with your body. Your mind (the CEO) gets to check in with your physical body to ensure that it is taken care of. For instance, your mind decides if the body is getting the optimal level of rest and optimal level of exercise. Your mind gets to ensure that the body is running smoothly, optimally tuned up for long-term success. When your physical body is healthy, it sets yourself up for sustained success.
- The CEO can maximize results when he can empower the body of the organization, and even each employee. Similarly, your mind can empower your physical body and every cell of your body to get excited for the vision that you are creating for your life. This creates maximum results, faster towards creating the vision.
- And in the best organization, mutual care for the CEO will also come from the body of the organization - from the executives, the managers, and the people who work for her or him. The rest of the organization wants the CEO to be healthy and well, so that it can give clarity and directions for the organization! Your

body also gets to check in with the leader, too this way. Sometimes your body gets to ask your mind, how it is doing and lead the mind to take time off and rest as well. Your body can lead the mind to this state by turning the mind off through meditation, mindfulness practice, movement, and play.

- The CEO cannot micromanage everyone and everything and tries to control everything. That would exhaust the CEO and that would make the body of the organization very uncomfortable. Similarly, your mind, the CEO of yourself, gets to set high intentions and clear vision, then detach from the outcome each moment. This allows space for the human error of your body, as it lives towards the vision, to be a part of the journey. When things don't always go exactly as envisioned, your mind can regain its peace by detaching and surrendering.

My goal as a coach for my high-achievement-oriented clients is to help them access this self-leadership skills by following this format. This is the journey of my clients remembering who they really are and how powerful they really are. One of my clients, Austin, wrote in his testimonial after working with me, and it is clear that he was able to take back the leadership role of his own life. He wrote, "Through the work I did with Yuri, I can honestly say I'm an active participant in my own life again. I'm actively working on my relationship with my father and having a deeper connection to my wife than ever before. I do more with my friends and as my wife said to me the other day, you just seem calmer and easier to be around. I've recently taken a new job that I wouldn't have imagined possible prior to putting in the work with Yuri and I can say that I wouldn't have had the confidence to ask for what I wanted out of this new opportunity, and given all the uncertain in the world, I wouldn't have believed in myself enough to even entertain the opportunity," he continues, "outside of work, I feel like I've found a new relationship with my wife. I'm happy to say that I have a deep loving relationship with my wife that I'm actively deepening. My relationship with my friends is better than ever! I'm able to laugh confidently and rebuild the relationships with my friends that I've neglected. The best part is I've been able to redefine my own meaning of success and I'm confident that I'll be able to achieve the dreams that I never thought were possible before."

This is the power of taking the CEO position of your life by distinguishing the difference between the different roles your mind and your body plays in self-leadership. What this self-leadership of his own life leads to is his undeniable and renewed confidence. What becomes more possible with accessing this self-leadership is feeling empowered and unstoppable in every area of his life. What becomes more possible is deep fulfillment and joy, knowing that he is back in the driver seat of his life.

Automatic Nature of Thoughts

What can get in the way between your mind and your body working together to result in powerful self-leadership is when your automatic thoughts can dictate your actions, or your reactions. For effective self-leadership, one must become aware of the automatic nature of your thoughts, and to train or fire these thoughts discerningly.

In fact, humans have 50,000 to 80,000 thoughts a day. More than 95 percent of those thoughts are repetitive, automatic thoughts that keep you where you are rather than where you're headed. In his book *Happiness Hypothesis*, Jonathan Haidt explains how this works by using a metaphor of a rider for the conscious mind (intentional thoughts) and an elephant for the unconscious mind (automatic repetitive thoughts). The conscious mind is like a rider, who guides the elephant. Without the rider being present, or being the guide, the elephant would do whatever it wants, based on how it feels. Without the elephant, the rider would have a purpose and a vision, but wouldn't have the vehicle to get to it powerfully. And this offers the glimpse into why self-leadership is so crucial for creating any visions that can come to life. Without the CEO (your focused mind), the body will typically follow the unconscious mind or the emotions. This is the reason most people, when living without setting powerful intentions, may fall into habits that don't serve them. This is why the rider and the elephant need each other.

Choose Your Thoughts that Serve You, Let Go of Everything Else

To self-lead, consciously choosing the thoughts you want to focus on so that it can empower your body to take action toward your goals and vision is key. In that process, remember to let go of any *fun blockers*, or fears, or any disempowering thoughts. To summarize this chapter, we have discovered that self-leadership is the vehicle that will get you to your destination of your best self. When you take back the CEO chair of your own life, you get to access more fulfillment and confidence into your life.

Journaling

1. What does it mean to you to self-lead, or be the CEO of your life?

____

____

____

2. What are some ways that your CEO and your body come together or communicate with each other? (Earlier I mentioned I do yoga, journaling, and meditating to ensure my body and my mind are aligned. What are your ways of inviting alignment?)

____

____

____

3. What habits would you, as the CEO of yourself, point out to your current self as the fun blockers that are stopping you from your best self?

____

____

____

Self-leadership is accessed by creating a powerful vision and empowering your body through self-discipline. In the following exercises, you will have a chance to create a morning routine to support your daily level of discipline. If you can start the day with a sense of discipline, the entire day feels more powerful.

Exercise: Self- Leading Yourself to Successful Mornings

Pick and choose from the following (inspired by *The Miracle Morning* by Hal Elrod). I recommend you start with two or three, then add layers each week if you'd like.

1. **Becoming Present:** meditation, prayer, guided meditation, going to the beach or outside and sitting in nature. Recommended time to start this practice is about 5-10 minutes. I recommend you sit on the floor where it is quiet, and straighten your spine during the choice of your "silence."
2. **Affirmation**: Choose an affirmation a day, pick one for the week, or pick one for the month, or for ninety days. You may also do multiple affirmations each day. I recommend you say them out loud and tap into the emotion of *being* that affirmation. For instance, if your affirmation is "I am powerful!" say it as if you are the most powerful person in the Universe and say it with the emotion of already being powerful. Repetition is powerful, so you may set a timer for two minutes, and keep saying them over and over again.
3. **Visualization:** Live your ideal day and your ideal life in your mind each morning. Just daydream for a few minutes. You can also write it out. Just be sure you can see it clearly in your mind's eye.
4. **Movement**: MOVE. YOUR. BODY. Move your energy. Wake up your body. Get the blood flowing. Run, jog, do yoga, go to

the gym, stretch, dance, have sex, walk mindfully walk, walk in nature, etc.

5. **Reading:** Read something inspirational or a book that helps you powerfully expand and grow. Pick a number of pages or a number of chapters you'd like to commit to.
6. **Journaling**: Journal about three things you're currently grateful for. Or three things you're grateful for that are in your future. You can also free write—just write down whatever comes to mind. Pick a topic each day and journal about it.
7. **Gratitude:** Text/connect with 1-3 people every morning to genuinely thank them for being in your life. Write a loving letter to your future self, future significant other, future clients, future wealth, or future abundance—whatever you want to call them/it—as if they/it are already in your life.
8. **Breathing:** Breathing, also called *prana*, is our life force. So many times, we forget to connect back to our breaths to reclaim our power, calmness, and peace. Inhale deeply through your mouth, as if you're sucking in air through a straw. Then exhale everything out through your mouth. Do this about 30-40 times. Then pause.

Exercise: Design Your Morning Routine for the Next Seven Days

1. What time will you get up? Pick 3 activities from above and incorporate them into your morning for the next 7 days. Write out what that looks like below:

Example:

5:45 a.m.: Wake up

6-7 a.m.: Do yoga

7-7:30 a.m.: Shower, get dressed

7:30-8:30 a.m.: Meditate for ten minutes, visualize for ten minutes, do breath work, journal, make bed, or clean.

8:30 a.m. Start the day

Write yours here:

____

____

____

____

____

____

____

Can you commit to this routine for the next seven days and track your progress here? On a scale of 1-10, 10 being completed your morning routine powerfully, and 1 being not completed at all, rate yourself here.

Day 1: _____

Day 2: _____

Day 3: _____

Day 4: _____

Day 5: _____

Day 6: _____

Day 7: _____

How did you do? What reflections can you make about the last 7 days?

____

____

____

____

____

CHAPTER 7

IGNITING YOUR "WHY"

"Take it,
take my hand.
I got you."
infinite love,
Universe
— y.c.

Dear amazing human being, do you know your "why" in everything you do? What is your "why" behind choosing the avatar for your best self? What is your "why" of accessing self-leadership to get to that version of yourself? What is the inner fire that drives you toward that best version of yourself?

Finding your *Why*

"I want to find my why. I want to know my purpose in life." My clients often initially say. Inspiring visionaries and leaders, such as Steve Jobs and Martin Luther King, Jr., all knew something powerful that made them the great leaders they were. That something is understanding the importance of letting people know the purpose and the intention behind why they are doing what they're doing, rather than just what they are doing. And how does knowing your why impact your overall happiness and wellbeing? Researchers in the positive psychology fields find that people who find meaning, or purpose in life tend to experience less pain, depression, and anxiety, directly increasing overall happiness and wellbeing. In other words, when you focus on finding out your why, many of your problems may become non-problems because now you have a much bigger mission that energizes you.

As we talked about in the last chapter, self-leadership, is where your mind leads the body to take action toward the vision. In a sense, your mind gets to be the CEO, or gets in the driver's seat. If your mind is the driver, then your body is the car that it drives. And within that vehicle, there is a force that makes that vehicle continue to move forward, and that is that engine. Imagine that *that engine, where fuel turns into energy*, is your purpose. When the purpose is clear, the internal motivation gets activated and the ride in the vehicle toward the destination becomes an enjoyable, powerful ride. To seek your purpose, think about the intention you are putting behind these actions.

Story of J.F.K and the Janitor at NASA

There is a story of J.F.K. visiting NASA in 1962, when he was touring the space station. He came across a man who was mopping the floor, and J.F.K. asked the man, "Hi what are you doing working here so late?" The janitor answered, "Mr. President, I am helping put a man on the moon." This is a great story about finding purpose and a vision. Many think that our purpose has to be something massive, but the *purpose* of the purpose is so that people can feel like they are part of something bigger than themselves: a bigger vision, a bigger mission, and a bigger impact. Even though this man was cleaning the floor of NASA, his purpose for being there wasn't to just clean the floor. He was clear on the purpose of his bigger vision, which was to put a man on the moon. That was his *why* and what inspired him to get up and show up to work every day. That was his engine for life. That was his reason for making his life feel meaningful.

Listen to the signs from the Universe

Oftentimes, the clues to your *purpose* happens easily when you follow your joy and that natural pull to do something. Mark Zuckerberg, the Founder of Facebook, said that he wasn't really trying to find his *purpose*, when he created Facebook. He just wanted to create something that connected people using the Internet, as he saw that as a gap he could close for his community. His "why" was to connect people, and in following that pull to create something for fun, he was able to create what we now know as Facebook. Now his vision for the world to be connected.

For me, all my life, I have been passionately curious about why people do what they do, why some people live a happy life, and some don't. From this natural pull, I write, I coach, I speak, and I create. Today, my vision is for people to live with more laughter, oneness, vulnerability and ease (L.O.V.E.) in their lives.

To find your *why,* be open to the natural flow of the Universe to unfold for you. Had Mark Zuckerberg never ended up at Harvard where he naturally discovered the need for people to connect over the Internet, he might not have created Facebook. Sometimes the events that naturally and effortlessly unfold for you in your life are leading you to your *why.* Sometimes they are direct signs of inspiration or intuition, sending you a dream, or sending messengers into your world to reflect your talents to you.

Start by asking some of these questions for yourself. Have you ever been repeatedly complimented regarding certain abilities you have, even though it comes very natural to you? Do you find it super easy and effortless for you to engage in certain activities that others find difficult or not fun? Do you find yourself in flow, losing sense of time and self, over a long period of time when you do some specific things? Have you experienced inevitable hardships in your life that you feel like you were meant to learn something in those experiences, and when you overcame them, it changed you for the better? These are some questions you get to start asking yourself.

Reflecting without Judgment

Don't put too much pressure on finding the "right" purpose in a short amount of time. Humans come with many—even infinite—gifts. The one you decide to pay attention to, and water will blossom in its own divine time. You can't find a "wrong" purpose. If you feel like you truly have found the "wrong purpose," it is either not your actual purpose, or that very experience of finding the "wrong purpose" is the divine steppingstone toward your actual purpose that *will* lead to your soul-on-fire purpose. Check back in with the most primitive meter to see if you're on the right track—sometimes all you have to know is that it feels good doing it. Joy and feeling good are your birthrights. Happiness is your birthright. If you know that in your heart, you will know to follow what makes you feel good and lights up your life.

"I'm not here to give you the standard commencement about finding your purpose. We're millennials. We'll try to do that instinctively. Instead, I'm here to tell you finding your purpose isn't enough. The challenge for our

generation is creating a world where everyone has a sense of purpose. Purpose is what creates true happiness"

- Mark Zuckerberg, at the *Harvard Commencement Address 2017*

Exercise: Journaling

1. What comes easy, effortless, and fun to you? (What do you do in your free time because it is easy, effortless and fun to you?) Name one or two activities here.

____

____

____

____

____

2. When you look at the world, what are some things you would give money or time to, if you had an infinite amount of money or abundance of time?

____

____

____

____

____

3. Why do you care about those causes? What experiences or memories from your own life inspired you towards those causes?

____

____

4. If you could choose the top 3 words to describe the ideal vision for the world, what would they be? (ex. For me, it is love, laughter, oneness, vulnerability, and ease)

5. Now take a moment to take out a piece of paper. Write this statement on the piece of paper. "Universe, today I am ready to receive clarity towards my vision of a purposeful life now." Now close your eyes, say this statement out loud. Take 10 minutes for the next to meditate with this intention to receive clarity towards your purpose in life. Then journal here what surfaced for you about your purpose and your vision. What became more clear for you?

CHAPTER 8

CREATING YOUR DESTINATION AS YOUR BEST SELF

All else aside,
stay passionate! About life,
about family, about your career, or
your creations; about your lover,
about your art, about your path and about your
ideas; about your failures and overcoming them,
about your fears and confronting them,
about your small to big successes and celebrating them.
Laugh loud, cry hard, love till the rawest
parts of your heart
dance and ache with the motions
of the waves and the movements of
the stars. Whatever you do,
pour your heart out and let
the world hear you.
Oh, dear, if nothing else,
stay passionate, stay passionate,
become a lover of life with me!

— y.c.

Creating the Road's Checkpoints

Now that you have defined the starting point, you have defined the vehicle and now the engine, and now we get to establish some specific goals to take you to the destination. And that destination isn't happiness or fulfillment; rather it is the best, divine version of yourself. And remember, it is the entire journey from your starting point to the destination of the best version of yourself that can offer you the gifts of joy, peace and fulfillment at any time.

And goals are just milestones along the way to your best self, to make sure that you're on the right path. So here, I offer you an opportunity to create some check points for yourself.

Exercise: Setting the Goals that Align with your Best Self

What was the name of your best-self avatar? ______________

What will you do to get closer to your best self in the next year?

Create a twelve-month plan for yourself in the categories of health, wealth, and relationships.

Your health goals can consist of your weight goals, diet goals, healing (physical, emotional, and spiritual) goals, morning and night routines, exercise goals, meditation goals, etc.

Your wealth goals can consist of how much income you want to bring in per month or year, or how much you'd like to save. It could also include how much you'd like to donate for a good cause, or how much you want to give. It could include assets you purchase and maintain, such as a home, a car, land, etc. It could also consist of your retirement plan, or saving for a specific goal, such as a trip, your wedding, etc.

Your relationship goals can include goals around romantic relationships, family, friends, and colleagues. It could include how often you want to put in the work toward the goals. For example, how often you will spend time with your parents, or will you make plans to visit your old friends in another state.

1. Twelve months from now your goals in:
   - Health________________________________
   - Wealth________________________________
   - Relationships___________________________
2. Six months from now your goals in:
   - Health________________________________
   - Wealth________________________________
   - Relationships___________________________
3. Three months from now your goals in:
   - Health________________________________
   - Wealth________________________________
   - Relationships___________________________
4. One month from now your goals in:
   - Health________________________________
   - Wealth________________________________
   - Relationships___________________________

These goals will powerfully serve you to ensure that you continue to move towards your best self. Now that you've created some checkpoints, let's take you to the next step: creating the rules, or standards, of the road.

CHAPTER 9
CREATING YOUR OWN RULES

Your soul, always,
already knows
what the best thing
to do is in every situation;
It just silently sits
and watches
how much your ego
can tempt you over
to do other things.
— y.c.

What Are Your Rules?

Clearly creating guidelines and standards for yourself can help you stay true to who you are, stay true and efficient towards the path to becoming your best self. There are two things you get to do to create this sense of alignment: 1) Get clear on your core values, and 2) Create a set of rules for yourself. But remember, these are *your* rules, no one else's.

Core values are the foundational beliefs that make up a person. They are powerful to set because they allow you to know what you're *aligning to, exactly.* Also they allow you to have what people call your *backbone.* I had a client who told me in the beginning of our working together, "I want to be known as someone who has a backbone. How do

I do this? How do I feel like I know what I stand for? How do I let go of the resentment I feel for those who I feel like screwed me over and walked all over me?"

The first thing I coached him to do was to create a set of core values for himself. This is how one creates the "spine" of who they get to be in this world, so they can stay strong and tall in what they believe in. And nothing is more powerful than knowing what you stand for; it sets a standard for yourself and those in your energy.

Some of my core values are:

- Creativity
- Integrity
- Growth
- Love
- Compassion
- Joy/happiness
- Ease
- Oneness
- Courage
- Vulnerability

When I have a conflict in my life, I can check into it and say, "Am I truly being in integrity and acting out of love? Does this contribute to my growth? Am I practicing compassion? Am I serving others?" Creating this list of core values clarify what one person will tolerate and not tolerate from and for themselves and others. Your core values get to be the guide you come back to when you have a decision at hand. Your core values will allow you to be more easily aware of the matters that do not align. Your core values clear your path toward your best self. The same client who came to me, after working with him for three months, he wrote this in his review of working with me "Most wouldn't believe me when I say, during my coaching with Yuri, she has helped me manifest new partnerships, build out incredible team members, advisors, and people are now magnetically coming to me, and wanting to help me build out my vision, instead of me having to seek out others." When you are aligned with your core values, peace, happiness, and miracles come naturally to you. You attract who you're being. Your core values remind you who you get to be.

Creating Your Own Standards

You, powerful being, also get to create rules that you govern by to create more flow into your life and to help you stay aligned to your core values. For example, when you're driving on the road, the value that the drivers want to stay aligned to is *safety*. To honor this core value of safety from the community of drivers, there are rules on the road. This provides specific guidelines for the drivers to create an environment of safety. It's the same thing for you. You may have a core value of integrity, for instance. To honor that core value, you get to have rules to help you stay aligned to that value of yours. So for instance, perhaps your "rule" to honor your value of *integrity* can be something like, "Work out everyday for 30 minutes." By setting a commitment for self, and honoring that rule, you are in the practice of building integrity with yourself.

Here are some rules I have for myself:

1. Wake up before 7 a.m.
2. Exercise for at least one hour daily.
3. Meditate daily for at least ten minutes.
4. Meditate for an extended amount of time (30 min to an hour) once a week.
5. Read or learn something new every week for at least 3-5 hours.
6. Connect with nature at least 3 times a week.
7. Practice yoga at least 5 times a week.
8. Treat each person with kindness and compassion as best as I can.
9. Create something new every day.
10. Call and connect with my mom at least once a week.

These rules are more specific and detailed plans to support me in staying aligned to my core values. For instance, I know that getting up before 7 a.m. and exercising daily allows me to stay aligned to my core values of "ease and growth" in my life. Or when I meditate for ten minutes a day, it helps me stay aligned to my values of "love, compassion, oneness" (and many more.) And when you create and stay in integrity to your core values, you also get to feel good knowing that you are honoring the values most important to you. In that, you get to feel happier and at peace, because deep down, you know you are living toward the standards that you set for yourself. Side effect of living aligned to your core values? Your confidence soaring, again.

And by the way, falling out of alignment or not honoring your own rules that you set doesn't make you *wrong or bad.* You just become misaligned, and your manifesting powers decrease. And so, regularly, you get to tune back in. "Okay, I have fallen away from my alignment, and my alignment comes from staying in my lane with my core values." When you fall out of alignment, acknowledge the "violation" of your own rules rather than being hard on yourself. This process gets to be the reference point and the training ground for your self-discipline also. My client within just a few weeks of working with me based on tuning himself back to alignment, he started attracting so many people that shared the same core values as him, and he started to create an abundance of opportunities and money within weeks. His magnetic powers increased when he stayed in alignment.

Now it's your turn.

Exercise 1

What are your top ten core values? List them below.

1. ______________________________
2. ______________________________
3. ______________________________
4. ______________________________
5. ______________________________
6. ______________________________
7. ______________________________
8. ______________________________

9. ______________________________

10. ______________________________

Exercise 2

Write out ten rules for yourself that you'd like to follow for the next 3 months to help you stay in alignment and disciplined.

1. ______________________________
2. ______________________________
3. ______________________________
4. ______________________________
5. ______________________________
6. ______________________________
7. ______________________________
8. ______________________________
9. ______________________________
10. ______________________________

CHAPTER 10

ACCESSING A CREATOR MINDSET

Dear Soul,

Create for me!

With love,

Universe

— y.c.

Free Yourself from a Scarcity (Fear-Based) Mindset

How often do you ask yourself questions like, "Why don't I have that yet?" or "Why is this happening to me?" Or have you ever felt upset that you really wanted something, whether it is money, promotion, relationship, or financial milestone, and you realized you're not there yet? What would open up for you if you were to shift from noticing not what's happening to you or what's missing from your life, to noticing what is already abundant in your life that you get to be grateful about?

Recently, I was invited to dinner where my hosts invited me to give thanks with them at the table before we ate. I realized I hadn't expressed gratitude before a meal in a long time and remembered how powerful it is to do so! This experience reminded me that there is still so much I take for granted every day because I am so abundant and get "used to it" that I just simply forget to appreciate every little thing. How amazing is it that I had an abundance of food and water available to me for as long as I have lived? How amazing is that I had an abundance of clean air available to me without skipping a day? This sudden realization made me feel like a queen—"Wow! I am *so* abundant."

And a creator mindset is when you are in tune with the abundance of the Universe. The more you get to tune into the mindset of a creator that you already are, you get to experience more flow and fulfillment in your life. Creativity cannot exist in the opposite spectrum of creator mindset, which is a fear-based mindset. Happiness, joy, freedom, peace and flow also cannot exist in a fear-based mindset. Therefore, creativity often coexists with happiness, joy, freedom, peace and flow.

When you access your creator mindset, you are just coming back to what's already most innate, easy, and natural for you. As you remove more of the "fun blockers" from your life, which are your fears and limiting beliefs, you start to remember and access the powerful creator within you more and more. So how do you know that you've entered the bubble of your creator mindset?

You know you're accessing your creator mindset when:

- You feel light, free, and joyful.
- You don't identify your worth in relation to your creations. You are the creator, not your creations. Your worth is not measured by how much money you have or make, your relationship or marriage, your kids' success, or anything else. These are your creations; your worth as a creator is immeasurable and infinite.
- You recognize and are grateful that your body is a vehicle of your soul, and you choose to cherish and take care of it.

- You know that you have the ability to create your thoughts and emotions at any time, therefore you lead yourself to more creative and abundant emotions (joy, freedom, peace, optimism) any chance you get.
- Your gap between your words and your actions are slim to none. You honor your words because fully understanding the power of words in creating your reality.
- You fully trust that the Universe is working for you, not against you.
- You are aware that there are no absolutes; there is no good, bad, wrong, or right. You recognize these are human-made categories that do not apply to a creator mindset.
- You create moments, new creations, thoughts, emotions, and actions with *an intention.*
- You are open to learning continuously and inspiring others.
- You don't judge other creators or their creations. You view other creators as artists of life and their creations as miracles.
- You are freely accessing and giving love.
- You have an abundance of vibrant energy.
- You are not affected by how others view you or your creations. You are in joy of being alive and being a creator.
- You are overflowing and you have more than enough to give and share your excess love to others.

- You are beyond just surviving and constantly in a creating mode so you are feeling abundant in all directions of your life.
- You easily and effortlessly access numerous solutions for every challenge.
- You embrace adversities as gifts of lessons.
- You have fun tapping into more possibilities all the time.
- You lead with "I can."
- You have internalized anything is possible because you are fully in ownership that you have the power to create anything.
- You are overflowing with gratitude.
- You naturally magnetize and invite amazing new resources, opportunities, connections, and love to help you create your vision.

In the next section, I will share stories about how having this creator mindset can empower you to create the reality of your dreams and live in abundance.

Creating an Empowering Life Through an Empowering, Possibility-Oriented (Creator) Mindset

Amy Purdy had a 98% chance of dying. Amy was a nineteen-year-old massage therapist with a passion for snowboarding when she fell ill with meningitis. While battling this disease, she lost the functions of her spleen and one kidney, and she lost both of her legs.

For most of her life, Amy had dreamed of traveling the world and snowboarding. What story do you think she created about her life after losing both of her legs?

In a *Sports Illustrated* interview, Amy was quoted as saying she was "grateful to be alive."

She said she had to ask herself, "This is my situation, what can I do?"

So she started to snowboard with her prosthetic legs. The legs didn't work for her when she tried to snowboard, so she had to work directly with the leg maker to create legs that fit her and her passion. As a result, she became the World Champion in the Paralympic Games. She also became a motivational speaker, inspiring people worldwide to live their wildest dreams and passions. She started a non-profit, *Adaptive Action Sports*, to aid other athletes training for the Paralympic Games; in fact, this organization contributed toward the category of snowboarding becoming a part of the Paralympic Games for the first time. Amy has also modeled and danced on *Dancing with the Stars*!

Amy could have created a different story. Accessing her creator mindset, she didn't let her thoughts go there. But... what if she had fallen into her fear-based mindset instead? Let's look at the differences in these two potential stories.

Facts:

Amy Purdy's legs got amputated due to her illness.

Her Disempowering Fiction could have been:

I cannot believe I lost my legs at only nineteen. This doesn't happen to anyone but me. I have the worst luck. I can never travel the world and snowboard anymore. I can't believe this is happening to me. My life is over. The Universe is against me.

Based on this perspective, she could have believed this about herself:

I am not deserving of following my passions in life.

God doesn't love me.

I have the worst luck.

I can't do anything.

Rules about life she could have created based on this story:

I am never going to snowboard again.

I am never going to try anything I love to do because it will never work out.

I am depressed.

Instead, accessing her creator mindset, her empowering fiction became:

I cannot believe I lived with only a 2 percent chance of survival! I am so glad they make prosthetic legs. I can still snowboard and travel as long as I make prosthetic legs that allow me to snowboard and travel. I'll have to figure out how to since those are my passions. I am starting a new life, and I will figure out my new circumstances.

Based on this creator perspective, she believes this about herself:

I am so lucky.

I am so grateful.

I am creative and can problem-solve.

I am an athlete.

Rules about life she created based on this story:

Anything is possible!

Circumstances do not dictate anyone's life.

There is always a way.

I am the creator of my own story!

Can you see how the same situation can be looked at completely differently and have an amazingly different outcome? What would you have chosen?

Let's try this with your own life examples.

Exercise

Think of an incident that made you feel disempowered. Then create a new empowering, creator-mindset based alternative for your life fiction and rules.

Facts:

What happened? What are just the facts of what happened?

____

____

____

Disempowering Fiction (Stories):

What are the immediate stories you made about this situation?

____

____

____

What are some stories you made up about who you are based on those stories?

____

____

____

What are the rules you either created or reinforced from those stories? (What could you have believed about yourself based on the disempowering story?

____

____

____

Review: Put on a different pair of lenses.

Now review the stories from #2. Out of those stories, scan to see if there are any of your own expectations that you created for that other person or about the situation. Look for words like "should" or "I wish." Also look for words like "always" or "never." Of these stories, which do you know to be 100 percent true?

____

____

____

New Empowering Fiction:

If you had to write a new creative and alternative story for this same situation that empowers, rather than disempowers you, what would it be?

____

____

____

What are some stories you can make up about who you are based on these stories?

____

____

____

What are some rules you can create or reinforce from this new story about your life?

____

____

____

Abundance Exercise

List 5 things that you are currently abundant in right now.

1. ________________
2. ________________
3. ________________
4. ________________
5. ________________

CHAPTER 11

ACTIVATING YOUR BEST SELF

Start
every morning with,
'What gift
can i bring
to the world today?'
— y.c.

What New Possibilities Will You Create?

With the mindset of a creator, abundance of new possibilities become open and available to you. Let's dream and create for a second: what new realities are possible for you that were not available for you before? What new unimaginable adventures, experiences, and connections are possible that were not real to you before? Knowing that you have the power to create and tune into any reality you desire, if you choose to, what will you tune into to ensure you live a life full of joy and peace?

So far in this book, we have talked about how you are a miracle, that you can create your new identity and empowering mindset from scratch if you want to in the journey towards your best self. One thing you get to remember is this. **You always have a choice to start over and start creating again.** You can be the author of your life at any time that you choose and start writing a new story. And by doing that, while not focusing on what was, but focusing only on what's possible, a whole new field of possible realities becomes wildly available to you that you haven't even considered.

You can do and be whatever you want, whenever you want. You create the rules and values. When I tell my clients that for the first time, they feel perplexed.

Their ego starts to freak out. "That is not possible! I am so stuck in this situation. There are no other ways!" their ego screams as it tries to protect itself. Our egos want to keep us safe: safe from failure, safe from humiliation, safe from change, safe from the unknown, safe from growth. It wants to keep us where we are because it is working for us in some ways. Our egos care more about making sure we don't "look bad" than exploiting our human potential. Our egos disconnect us from the real reason we do what we do—our soul's purpose—because it is so busy trying to make sure we please other people and protect the egos.

The ego's intention isn't malicious, but if we let it lead our lives, and we stop dreaming and envisioning new possibilities, we will become trapped in the ego's illusion of safety, and we end up playing small. We end up settling for a job we hate. We end up settling for a lifestyle that doesn't serve us. We end up settling for a relationship that doesn't work. We end up blocking out infinite possibilities and staying with the same routine, in the name of safety and protection. Then we end up living the same year forty, fifty, or sixty times until we retire. Then one morning, we wake up wondering what happened to our precious life. The presence of our egos dominating our lives, creativity, peace, harmony, and happiness are often sacrificed.

So let go of your ego! Give yourself permission to start dreaming like a child again!

It is never too late to start dreaming and creating new visions for your life. Entering into your creator mindset, and accessing infinite possibilities is fun and exciting. It is like entering a new video game. You can lead your life to any direction you want. The only person stopping you is, you. You have the control. Get out of your own way. Lead yourself to believe new possibilities and realities are available for you outside of those you are living. There are possibilities you have not even thought of yet. Consider that anything is possible.

And if you have a hard time believing this, don't forget: You are already miraculous. You are powerful. You have been creating the reality you're in all your life. That is who you really are. You are a creator.

Igniting the Engine...Let's Go!

Now that you've identified where you are, where you are headed (your best self), your core values and the rules to get there, your vehicle to get there, and the engine for that vehicle, you are ready to go on this journey towards your best self. You are ready to get on the journey where happiness, joy, and peace are available for you every moment. Vroom *vroom*! Ignite your engine for this joyride toward your most fulfilled life!

We explore and expand the corners of various concepts around how to access happiness, starting with freedom, then expansion, expression and finally connection.

The next section in Part II, is about how to achieve emotional and spiritual freedom towards your happiness.

Once you are able to truly free yourself from all those that previously held you back, you will be able to access the next phase of the transformation process, which is the phase of *expansion.*

Then in Part III, as a free particle can move and expand into any direction, expansion is the theme. Expansion is the natural outcome when you access and lead with your creative mindset.

Then in Part IV, self-expression is highlighted as a key component of living a happy, fulfilled life.

Lastly, Part V, connection as a powerful ingredient to your long-term happiness and fulfillment is revealed.

So how do you ignite the engine for this powerful activation?

It starts with your decision to commit to this version of you. Here is your contract for your journey toward your best self, to solidify this commitment for you.

I, __________, powerfully commit to taking this joy ride by hopping in this vehicle toward the best version of myself. I am leaving all my roadblocks behind me. I commit 100 percent with every cell in my body to step into my best version of myself.

Signature: ____________________ Date: ____________________

Ready? Let's go!

Part II

UNLEASHING YOURSELF TOWARDS FREEDOM

CHAPTER 12

SHEDDING THE MASKS

Sometimes I dance to the
melodies of loud silence;
My heartbeat creates this
rhythm that makes me feel alive
my untamed movements
bring light into
tangled parts of my heart.
There is an echo of my own humming
that reminds me of
my own voice.
Sometimes I dance to the
melodies of my silence;
It brings out the loudest
parts of me
that only yearn
to be heard.
— y.c.

By 2020, we have all been exposed to the experience of wearing a mask due to the global pandemic that's affected most of us. I've heard many people share that wearing these masks for a long time can feel stuffy, uncomfortable and restricting. Here's the thing though. Unrelated to the physical masks that we wear, many of us have been wearing masks longer than prior to 2020. Many of us have been wearing these different kinds of masks that have been hiding and suffocating our true authentic selves for a while.

I'll share a story about a *mask* that I wore for a long time. I wore the mask of a "party girl" most of my college years and in my early 20's. While this mask served its purpose, such as giving people the illusion that I fit in and that I was "cool," deep down, I felt restricted and my deeply creative, unique and artistic soul felt trapped. At parties or bars, I bonded with people by talking about things I really never cared about that much, such as how many shots of tequila I had taken the night before, what happened at that one party when that one guy did this, or what my favorite drink is at the bar down the street. Talking about these things made me feel relevant and cool in the moment, but deep down, I felt lonely. Back in those years, I never talked about my passion for poetry, my deep love for positive psychology, my big dreams of becoming an author or becoming a speaker to impact the world positively. I didn't talk about my unique insights I'd find from reading all my textbooks (yes, I read most of my textbooks) or my infinite curiosity for the universe and all the cosmic wonders outside of the Earth. I never talked about the blog I had started on positive psychology with an intention to inspire others or the poems that I posted there. I stayed anonymous even when I would post my writing and thoughts on my blog. I didn't talk much about my favorite TedTalk that I had just listened to, and how it inspired me to volunteer at a non-profit called *American Foundation for Suicide Prevention* for a few years. These things didn't seem "cool" and I didn't think anyone would care. I chose to talk about what seemed to matter to other people and wore this mask of being a "party girl." This gave me an opportunity to meet and drink with a lot of people and have many meaningless conversations; but I never got to be brave to be who I really was. And in return, they never got a chance to really get to know me. And this is why I felt lonely in this. And it was my own fault - I was not courageous enough to take my mask off, and say, this is who I really am underneath that "party girl" mask. I was self-sabotaging my own opportunities to be accepted and seen for who I was! Over the years, as I started to own these unique qualities, passions and dreams of mine, I started to let go of my mask of being just a *party girl.* I started to feel free and powerful standing tall in all that made who I really was. I became more and more comfortable in my own skin.

What masks are you wearing to hide your true powerful selves?

What about you? Do you ever choose to put a mask on because you don't want to look silly? Do you ever choose to not speak up and share what's really on your mind from the fear it will upset someone or that they will judge you? Do you ever find yourself putting on a show away from who you really are just to please others and fit in? What fears come up for you when you think about opening up and speaking your mind powerfully? Underneath the masks you wear, who are you really? What would it feel like to free yourself from these heavy masks? What fun, freedom and flow are these masks blocking you from truly having in life? What would it feel like to be emotionally, spiritually, and completely free by taking these masks off? What would it feel like to be seen, accepted and loved for who you really are?

Exercise: Removing Masks You Could Be Hiding Under

Before we go further, I invite you to take a minute to think about which masks you might be hiding behind. I've listed several below. Circle the ones that resonate with you.

Mask of "I never fail": A person wearing this mask is often playing small, has a fear of failure, might be avoiding taking responsibility and not exploiting their full potential. We are all supposed to fail along our journey! If you're not failing *ever*, it means you're never stepping outside of your comfort zone.

Mask of "Everything is fine": A person wearing this mask is pretending that everything is under control when they might be feeling out of control at times inside. This person might be not addressing and expressing their true emotions. A person might fear conflict or standing up for what they truly believe in.

Mask of "Party girl/boy or being cool": A person who wears this mask is focused on "looking good" and scared to "look bad." He or she might have a fear of not feeling accepted or being included.

Mask of "Mr. / Ms. Perfect": A person who wears this mask is critical and hard on him or herself. This can lead to inaction or procrastination.

Mask of "I am always being taken advantage of (Victim Mentality)": A person who wears this mask is in a blame mode and unable to take responsibility for the person's life. In the process, this individual easily gives away personal power that he, she or they have.

Looking at this list, I invite you to go inward, instead of outward. Which mask resonates with you the most? Or what other masks that are not listed here do you wear? And if you find yourself wearing any of these masks, why are you hiding? Why won't you show us how bright you can shine in your light? Why won't you let us see how magical you really are?

Side Effects of Masks: Shame & Imposter Syndrome

Some people are scared to access their real selves because they fear that they would be judged, ridiculed, cast out of their friends' groups, or whatever irrational fears come up. They secretly and silently ask themselves, "what if they find out who I really am?" or "what if they find out I am not as great as they initially thought I was?" This is where imposter syndrome can derive from. Imposter syndrome is when a person feels like a "fraud" because he or she fears that these masks that he or she wears don't really portray who they really are inside, and they are scared to be "found out." Because of this fear and shame around these masks that people wear, people often get stuck. They get stuck from trying new things, going after their dreams, starting that business, and so on. So, they continue to hide under their masks, rather than try anything new and risky that could make their masks fall off. But here's the thing. When you courageously take off the mask first and be loud and proud about who you really are, with all your brightness as well as your darkness, that fear falls away. Being vulnerable can make the masks that cause procrastination, inaction and feeling stuck fall away.

Vulnerability Lets the Soul Breathe

Here is what I have learned about us, humans, as I have coached and helped thousands over the years about their mindset. Secretly, people crave vulnerability. Why? It frees them from these masks, and it is lighter when they are free. And because they want connection. They want intimacy. And only when people are vulnerable with one another, authentic connection can be birthed. This is what I know from my experience of shedding my own masks over the years and becoming more and more raw and vulnerable: it takes practice being vulnerable before it gets easy, just like anything else, but the rewards of connection and freedom are well worth it. And even for me, there's always another layer that I can shed so I continue to go deeper in this journey of self-discovery. And to quote Moshe Dayan, "freedom is oxygen of the soul." So take off those masks. Be open. Be vulnerable. Let your soul breathe. It's time you free yourself.

Becoming A Free Spirit: What happens When You Drop Your Masks

"Dad, what is your one most important advice you'd give me in life?" I asked my dad two weeks before he passed away from his brutal battle with cancer.

"Ha, that's easy!" he replied. "Be a free spirit!"

So how do you become a free spirit? Once you ditch your masks that you hide under, you start to feel increasingly freer and lighter in your body. This is why I help my clients become aware and consciously drop these masks through helping them become more vulnerable and authentic. One of my clients, during our coaching, became inspired to go alcohol free for 2 months. When he decided to quit drinking, he had a rather unexpected concern. "I haven't told any of my best friends that I quit drinking for a while." I asked him, "Why haven't you?" He hesitated, and looked at me and said, "I am scared that I am going to lose my friends because they would think I am weird for not drinking." So instead of holding on to this story he was creating in his mind, I invited him to drop his "cool guy who drinks beer" mask and tell his friend exactly what he told me: how he was scared to tell his friends because he fears that he will lose them as friends. At first, he was hesitant, but I got a nice text message from him the following afternoon. "You wouldn't believe what happened! I really thought our friendship would be over, but by telling him my exact things that were on my mind, he assured me that we would be friends regardless and that we can always find something else to do other than drink beer!" What I sensed in him at that moment was relief and freedom. Relief came from the fact that he didn't actually have to worry about not being accepted as who he really was and becoming; and I sensed that his freedom came from being free of his mask of "being the cool guy."

That day, what my client became is wide steps towards becoming a free spirit. It's impossible to be happy and fulfilled without feeling a sense of emotional and spiritual freedom. And what it took for me to become a free spirit meant I had to ditch my masks and open myself up to being vulnerable and courageous to expand and breakthrough my beliefs that were limited, just like my client did on that call with his friend. What are some signs that you are on your path to becoming or you are a free spirit?

Here are the characteristics of a free spirit:

- Speaking your truth without worrying if others will accept or judge you
- Being open to hear others' radical truth without judgement

- Being vulnerable
- Being unattached to the outcome
- Living a life on your own terms
- Choosing to do something because it aligns with your terms, not because everyone else is doing something
- Defining your own ideas of success and happiness
- Being a radiant light and not letting anyone dim your light
- Following your inner guidance towards joy, peace, and love

Happiness is the nectar of your soul when your soul experiences true freedom. So start to shed your masks. Your soul will appreciate you for it.

Journaling Exercise

1. What masks do you wear over your authentic self?

____

____

____

____

____

____

____

2. What has been the cost of wearing this mask? What parts of you have you been hiding?

3. What would it feel like to take off this mask and be your authentic self?

CHAPTER 13

FREEING YOURSELF FROM JUDGMENTS

The other side of the
thick heavy line
called fear
is a beautiful place
called being
vulnerable.
If you dare,
meet me there.
— y.c.

Judgment: Your Finger Pointing Back at You

When was the last time you judged others? What was the particular trait you judged them on? I remember, my mom once told me something really profound that changed the way I understood judgement forever. I was about seven years old. She told me… "Yuri, [in Korean] Imagine that any particular traits of others that you talk about, judge or make fun of in this lifetime, are the very traits that you will be born with in your next life. So before you ever judge or make fun of someone for something, imagine first how you will feel when you have that same trait that you're talking about, and how you'd feel in your next life if someone made fun of you for that. It doesn't feel good, right? So if you make fun of someone for her disability, that is the same disability that you will be born with in your next life. If you judge someone for being too tall or short, you will be too tall or short in your next life. So be mindful who and what you talk about, make fun of and judge, knowing that you are making fun of yourself too." This was a life changing lesson for me as a child. I decided at an early age that I'd do my best at not judging others because, well, why would I? I am going to have that same thing I make fun of in my next life! And I know it wouldn't feel good for someone to make fun of me then! As a young child, I remember stopping and thinking before I made fun of someone, "how would that feel when I have that trait in my next life and someone made fun of me?" Over time, I realize that this was my mom's wise way of teaching me about empathy. And on a spiritual level, I understood that anything I do unto others will come back to me. The harm that I cause others, is the harm I cause myself. Have you ever made a judgement about someone based on their sexual orientation, appearance, the way that they raise their kids, or religion? Well now, whoever that is, imagine that is exactly the trait that you will be born with in your next life. Because of this, I started putting myself in others' shoes more often, instead of jumping to judgements.

I remember once I overheard a girl talking about another person that was in line in front of us at a party. She turned to me, even though I didn't know her very well, "that girl is way too skinny. She needs a burger." In that moment of her judgement, instead of continuing this chain of negativity, I wondered what this girl was going through in her own life that she felt that need to judge this stranger in front of us. In that moment, I poured her love. And I also became aware that her judgement of this person in front of us was probably her own projection of her own struggles with her own body image. I lovingly responded to her, "Hey, maybe she is working through some eating disorder or struggles that we aren't aware of. I hope she's healthy." With that, she quickly realized what she was doing, "wow, thanks for pointing that out." In that moment, I felt that I was able to turn a moment of continued judgement and gossip, into a powerful moment of compassion.

Judgement-free environment is absolutely necessary for transformation, love, connection, and freedom. For my clients, it is absolutely necessary that I set up the container for no judgement to support their transformation for this reason. And here's the thing. When you stop judging others, your own fear of being judged also dissolves away ironically. One traps him or herself, and no one else, by judging others. So instead of judging others, I have learned to train my eyes and my ears to look for and to notice amazing things about others. And maybe that's because I am still secretly thinking about what my mom said to me as a child.

Judgment Zone = Danger Zone for Growth & Joy

What's the *danger* in judging others? The most dangerous part about judging others is actually that we miss an opportunity to confront our own fears, our own areas of growth and our own chances to go inward to learn more about ourselves. Judgment distracts us from where the attention really needs to go towards: our own selves. So when you find yourself judging others, go within. That's where judgment comes from—within you, the part in your heart where fear still resides. Chances are, you are judging yourself on the same standards that you're judging others in, which becomes the source of your own insecurity and perfectionism. For example, that example of the girl judging another person in front of us in line based on her weight or her appearance, indicates that she might actually be struggling with her own insecurity around her own body. And instead of working through her own insecurity, it manifested as a judgement towards another person. Therefore, judgement that we hold for others shows us where we are still wounded and need healing. So the beautiful thing about your judgement towards others is that it shows you your next spiritual work is for *you*, not anyone else. For instance, I remember I once judged my ex-boyfriend for not calling me back when he said he would. My internal judgement started to say things in my mind like, "He's out of integrity! He doesn't keep his promises about calling me when he said he would." Then I had a moment of awareness that reminded me that every judgement is a reflection of myself and where I need to grow. Instead of staying in judging mode, I tried on this idea. "If I know that everyone is a reflection of my own being, who have I not called back, and where have I been out of integrity that way that this is being reflected back to me?" I started to scan my last few days. Oh gosh! I had totally spaced calling my mom back. She was in South Korea at the time, and I was in California, and we have a different time zone, so last time she called me I was half asleep. And I told her I'd call her back the next day. And I had totally spaced it. So instead of staying upset that he had not called, I took that time to call my mom back to restore my own integrity. By the time he remembered and called me, I was already happy, already feeling connected, and feeling love in my heart because I got to connect with my mom! In a way now, I was grateful for him, even in him not keeping his promise, because it gave me an opportunity to reflect on my own life and become better. And truly, learning about ourselves and evolving as a soul are really the only assignments that the Universe assigned us. Our job isn't to tell others where they need to grow, unless asked for it. So where judgement comes up, take the lesson that the judgement is teaching you about you, grow from it, thank it, then release it.

Judgment Is a Barrier

"Judgements prevent us from seeing the good that lies beyond appearances."
— Dr. Wayne Dyer

Judgment is a barrier that stops us from truly connecting with other souls; you can't love, inspire, or connect with someone when you're judging them. When you're judging others, it leaves room for zero compassion, zero understanding, zero empathy, and zero love for others. Judgement leads to disconnection and loneliness. Do you feel disconnected and lonely? Scan where you are judging others and try on what it would feel like in your body and in everyday life if you were to drop that judgement and pour them compassion instead. How would your life be different? For me, I found that freedom, happiness and creativity are what blossom in absence of judgements.

Releasing Anxiety Over Others Judging You

I often hear from my clients when I initially start working with them that they have an underlying fear of being judged or that they experience anxiety about what others think of them. Do you also ever find that you're being judged by someone else, and this causes you anxiety or stress? In those moments, notice that he or she is the one disconnecting and separating from the world. Know that they may be lonely in sitting with those judgements *of you*. Instead of reacting to their judgement and reinforcing the fear energy, just send them love. Send them compassion. They are reacting to their own fear. **Their judgement about you doesn't mean anything about you and has nothing to do with you. It only reveals their own areas that can be healed and freed more. It reveals where they get to go deeper in terms of *their* next spiritual homework toward *their* best selves.** What others judge you about doesn't change who you really are. Your soul is made of love. Don't let their fear affect you in a way that makes fear contagious. Love them and love them harder in the presence of their judgment toward you. In that moment of abundant love, you will free yourself. And maybe one day, your love will inspire them so much that they cast out their own fears and judgements too. And they, too, can achieve freedom through erasing judgment from their reality. Love *is* that powerful. Love *is* the cure for healing the judgement wounds for all.

Because of this, in the end, you get to thank the people you thought were judging you because they showed you how powerful you can be with your love energy even towards them. Then, there you are, back in gratitude, on your way to your inner peace and joy, embracing this power of yours.

Exercise

1. Scan your last week. What instances can you become aware of intentionally or unintentionally judging anyone, if any? Are there any that crossed your mind, even if you didn't tell anyone about it?

2. What could these judgements that you hold be teaching you, about you?

Chapter 14

Honoring your Truth

You are amazing.
You are unique.
You are a miracle.
So why on Earth
are you hiding?
— y.c.

Speaking your Truth

Do you ever hold back from telling your full truth? Your ego might come in and say, "*I always tell the truth!*" Hold on ego, there is no judgement here. You are infinitely loved and there's nothing to prove. Most people have been inauthentic about something at one point, whether intentionally or not. You know those moments where you have sugar-coated your deep emotions, whether it be deep love for someone or shame? Do you ever hide the authentic intensity of your emotions because you are scared of what people will think of you? Do you ever say, "I'm fine!" when someone asks you how you're doing, when you are actually feeling deeply empty inside?

Let me briefly share with you about my experience of losing my dad to cancer. At the time, my soul was in a dark place, riddled with fear and sadness. I was so afraid of losing my dad, and part of me was scared to share my deep emotions regarding the process. I was afraid people would think I was "too much" or "too emotional."

Then one day, I decided to open up about my experience. Instead of thinking about myself and what it could do to me, I thought about how my story could potentially help other people. After I started to share vulnerably on social media and to people, I got so many messages on Facebook and texts and people also starting to share about their experiences. They too, were going through an adversity of some sort and they appreciated that I shared openly. Many told me my story of strength and resilience also helped them in different ways. And I realized something powerful by surrendering into sharing: Truth doesn't need approval or permission. Truth just is. Truth is the frequency of love energy. And in that it is so powerful. I am sure I made some people uncomfortable by expressing the rawness of my experience. But I learned that if my truth makes others shrink, that was not my role to fix or manage.

Showing up authentically as yourself may not get everyone to agree with you or "like you." Think about it this way. There is simply no way with 7.5 billion people in the world, that *everyone* will agree with you or "like you." And *that's okay.* Imagine how exhausting it would be for your soul if you try to please everyone in the world. You will learn to *respect* yourself for showing up unapologetically as yourself.

Think of Lady Gaga. In a recent interview in an article called "Lady Gaga is a creation; but an authentic one" in *Today*, Lady Gaga admits she is an "odd person" in general. She openly admits and owns her past that led her to who she is, and all the eyebrow raising behavior that she's engaged in the past. Yet her fans *love* her because she stands in her truth and in her uniqueness. On Twitter alone, she has over 80 million followers and on Instagram, 41 million, having massive influence in the world.

Many creatives, entrepreneurs, and various types of creators, who openly honor and express their raw opinions and their truth through their work change and shift the world. People admire that they forgo the need to feel accepted, or fit in, while staying committed to their mission and individuality. You are robbing the world a chance to be wow'd by your uniqueness when you aren't being 100% authentic.

So I invite you to be open and let the world see you have strength and are grounded in your truth. When you have those quirky weird thoughts, talk about them; don't hide them. When you have unpopular or unique thoughts and you know in your heart it's the right thing to do, voice them and explain why; stand up for what you believe in that contributes to the betterment of the world. You get to free yourself, and access more happiness now, through your courage to be authentic.

Exercise

1. Can you recall a time that you didn't tell your full truth out of fear?

____

____

____

____

____

2. Can you identify what that fear was? If you were to speak your full truth despite your fear, what would become available for you?

CHAPTER 15

FREEING YOURSELF FROM PERFECTIONISM

You can't chase
what you already are,
perfection,
you are,
darling.
— y.c.

Do you have Perfectionist Tendencies?

Have your desires to "get things right" or "get things perfect" ever stopped you from taking action at all, leading to procrastination? Yes, me too. I call myself the "recovering" perfectionist. Even writing this book, my perfectionist tendencies started to creep in. And one day, I just had to choose that my purpose and my reason for writing this book - to be of service to others - was simply greater than my ego's need to be perfect. And look…no one is perfect. We all have lopsided body parts. We all have different birthmarks, freckles and scars. They are what makes us real and *absolutely stunning*. We all fail at one point, and we all win at another point. We all break down sometimes, and we all break through other times. We hurt sometimes, and we all heal sometimes. This is what makes us human. Being hyper focused on a society's standard of "perfect" is a recipe for unhappiness. Every time anyone inches closer to their ideal of perfection, that target moves two inches further away. Many feel unhappy for a long time chasing this ideal of perfection that keeps moving. It is a target that is impossible to get right. But beautiful beings, let me tell you something that you won't want to hear yet. You are already perfect.

"Perfectionism is self-abuse of the highest order."
— Anne Wilson Schaef

Letter to You, with Perfectionist Tendencies

Dear Perfectionist,

I know you because I have too, been you. You are a different breed than most. This is what occupies your brain: "You are doing a good job, but you are never doing enough." "You are amazing, but everyone knows you could have done a better job." "If you work harder, and harder, you can be finally worthy of love." So I gift you this.

What you need to hear today is this:

"You are allowed to screw up."

"You are allowed to get messy."

"You are allowed to be completely, utterly broken, because you will come back stronger, always"

"You are loved, even when you are not perfect."

"You don't have to be happy all the time."

"You are worthy of love."

You can't chase what you already are

A few weeks ago, I had a session with one of my high achieving, brilliant, male clients. He had just shared how he thinks he has been chasing perfectionism all his life. He took on conditioning from his dad at an early age that excellence is necessary for him to be validated. He said that he was exhausted from trying to have his life together and perfect for him.

I asked him, "If I share something with you, could I request that you just try your absolute best to sit with what I'm saying and let it get to your heart?"

"Sure," he said, not knowing what's coming.

I asked to confirm, "Do you promise? Even if it feels uncomfortable, and even if it feels like every cell in your body screams 'that's not true!'..?"

"Yes," he said, puzzled at this point.

"Ok, thank you for trusting me," I said, taking a deep breath in, getting grounded so I can speak directly from my heart.

Connected to my heart, I slowly exhaled, then I said,

"You... are perfect. All humans are perfect already."

His eyes swelled up, and I checked in with my heart, and continued.

"You can't chase what you already are. You get to relax now knowing the chase is over."

And he let his tears fall for the first time in a long time. He hadn't shown emotions like this in over a year, he later admitted. I felt his heart crack open. The following session, it was no surprise to me when he told me that his wife and him had one of the most connecting conversations in over a year. And that he did the unthinkable - ask for help! He said he felt closer to his wife than ever before, doing he thought would make him look weak, ironically.

My Story of Overcoming Perfectionism

I flushed down the shame. I threw up again. My obsession to be perfect and be skinny was taking over my life for about 6 weeks or so back in 2006. This shame I felt immediately after I'd purge was reaffirming that fact. What was I doing? How did I get to this point?

In my later teens and my early 20's my goal was to be perfect. In college, I wanted to get perfect grades, party, be a social butterfly, be skinny and fit, be liked, be in a sorority, be in an honor society, and be funny, and more - the list just kept growing. The result of this obsession with being perfect overworking and overachieving for my worth. And I assumed that at the time that worth came from checking off that list, not from within. And this perfectionism got me good grades, two degrees in 4 years, lots of party friends, and lots of partying and drinking, but that subtle voice in the back of my mind that said "you're still not enough" remained. From my one-hundred-and two-pound body, I would say, "Yep, everything is fine!" But I wasn't. When I looked in the mirror, I wasn't skinny enough, pretty enough, or fit enough. This idea of *being perfect* was so overpowering that I started rejecting my food.

Thankfully, I made a decision a few weeks into it to stop. But many do not. In fact, according to the *Association of Anorexia Nervosa and Associated Disorders*, more than 30 million people in the U.S. suffer from eating disorders. While eating disorders are not always linked to perfectionism 100%, *the World Health Organization* confirms that perfectionism-related anxiety disorders are rapidly increasing in general. And for me while my temporary habit of rejecting food didn't manifest into a full eating disorder or anxiety disorder, it very well could have; also, perfectionism still manifested in many areas of my life and haunted me away from living a life that I was excited to live. Today, I can say I have learned to love myself for my perfectly imperfect-self. Today, I genuinely love myself.

"I love myself; therefore, I attract loving people into my life."
— Bob Proctor

Power of Mindfulness as a Cure for Perfectionism

For my clients who are often trapped in the ideals of perfectionism, I highly, wholeheartedly recommend and guide them to mindfulness practices such as breath work, meditation, and yoga. I help them to incorporate mindful practices into their lives. In 2008, I was again trying to do 234,453 things in one day. Then, in my hurried, non-present state, I got into a car accident. Looking back, that accident was the Universe helping me by forcing me to *slowwwww downnnnnn.* I was prescribed pain meds and muscle relaxers for my neck and back, but neither sat well in my stomach, so I was in even more pain. Realizing I needed a holistic healing just in case this pain become chronic, I took myself to my first yoga class. Through yoga, I started my journey of accepting myself and accepting my body as it is, creating inner happiness, and finally freeing myself from chasing perfection.

When I started to do yoga and practice mindfulness, I started to remember how miraculous my body really is. The way it can move, stretch, and bend is truly miraculous. We are such divine creations and creatures. When we start to pay attention to our breath, you realize how amazing it is every one of your breaths is the reason you are alive, yet our breathing is happening effortlessly for us. How awesome is that? How perfectly engineered are we?

Perfectionism blinds us from many wonders of life. When we are striving for perfect "things" and "conditions," we forget to marvel at the beauty that each moment already offers us. We get excited when we find four-leaf clovers, which are technically the imperfect, mutant clovers and the weird ones, don't we? They are beautiful in their imperfections. If we can truly surrender to where we are right now, and appreciate the perfection of this present moment, we get to have more peace and joy in our hearts. In the next chapter, we go deeper into the healing and freeing benefits of mindfulness.

Exercise

1. How has perfectionism affected you in your own life?

____

____

____

____

____

2. What has been the benefits of keeping this perfectionism around, and what has been the cost?

3. What new amazing possibilities for you could emerge in your life if you were to let go of your perfectionism today?

Affirmations to release perfectionism from your body and your mind:

- I am already perfect. I can't want what I already am.
- I am perfect in my outer self, my inner self, and everything in between.
- I am exactly where I am supposed to be.
- I love and accept myself.
- I trust the Universe to accept me for all I am.
- I am beautiful.

CHAPTER 16

BEING PRESENT

Every day,
every moment,
every connection,
is a gift,
a new opportunity,
a new beginning.
— y.c.

The Art of Doing Nothing: Meditation

Are you a human "doing," or do you often allow yourself to be a human "being"? Do you take time to come back to the present moment, relax or renew your body and soul? Or do you ever worry or get anxious about the future? Do you ever get depressed thinking about your past? Are you type A, and have a difficult time relaxing or being fully present? Well, if you're wondering how I know all this, this was exactly how I felt many years ago. It was through consistent practices of yoga and mindfulness that started to change my life.

Let me tell you about a time that I visited the Deer Park Monastery for their day of meditation. One of the monks, during a little talk on mindfulness, joked, "Really, monks are just really good at being lazy." This made me giggle a little. I thought, what a true statement! Being lazy was impossible for me when I used to chase perfectionism. I used to rather run 5 miles than sit and do nothing. Through my consistent practice of meditation, I learned that doing nothing is, ironically, sometimes the key to getting more things done; doing less or doing nothing is a form of art in itself.

In those moments where you feel like you're constantly doing so much, can you come back to the present moment, and allow yourself to just be a human-being, not human-doing? Can you take the time to consciously relax and reflect to let go of the idea that being busy is the only key to getting more done? Can you let the waves and trembles of your mind calm down to a still state?

When your mind is still and clear, that is when you can find the true and clear reflection of yourself and get a glimpse of your soul. Have you ever tried to look at a reflection of yourself in the turbulent waves of the ocean? What about a lake or a pond? Why is it that they are both bodies of water, yet one can show you the reflection of your face, and another cannot? It is also through the calmness of your being that you can truly get a moment to truly reflect on yourself. Achieving that clarity of seeing who you really are right now, and realizing you are perfect as you are, is the first step toward true self-love and acceptance. When you reflect, relax, and renew regularly and consciously, it opens up space in your life for you to grow, realign, and find peace within. So don't forget to be a human-being, not just a human doing. We are perfect, exactly where we are, as we are. And in this knowing, we get to create our own happiness knowing we already have all we need, and the chase for perfectionism and other not-being-present symptoms rest in peace forever.

Anxiety: When you're stuck in the future

What is anxiety? According to American Psychology Association, people with anxiety have tension and repetitive intrusive worries that also result in physical symptoms such as increased blood pressure, sweating, increased heartbeat and dizziness. When anxiety is the primary symptom, it can be called generalized anxiety disorder; but anxiety can also become the symptom of other mental disorders, such as obsessive compulsive disorder, post-traumatic stress disorder (or PTSD), phobias and many more. Anxiety affects over 40 million adults, just in America alone, according to statistics by Anxiety & Depression Association. That's roughly 1 in 5 people in America. Globally, according to the World Health Organization, over 300 million people are affected by anxiety.

In the spiritual realm, anxiety occurs when there is a disconnection between your body and your mind. Your body is in the present moment, and your mind is stuck in the future or a disempowering potential imagined situation that hasn't happened yet. Dr. Wayne Dyer talks about how there's no reason to ever worry in one of his talks. He says if it is in your control, do something about it; if it is not, why worry since you can't do anything about it anyway? So come back to now where your physical body is. Reunite your body and your mind in the present moment, and let go of everything else if you find yourself stuck, worried or anxious. You deserve to be free.

Freeing Yourself From Stories about Your Past

Any fear you feel, is you choosing to live in your past. Why? Because if you were being present and accessing your creator mindset, you probably wouldn't choose to create and feel a negative emotion, would you? You'd probably choose to feel one of the emotions of a creator instead, such as joy, peace, love, or willingness. When you're thinking about what happened in the past, you are missing out on what's going on right now. You are trying to control what's not controllable anymore—history of what happened.

Freedom Through Staying in the Present Moment

True freedom comes from being in the moment. Life is happening now, and nowhere else. Being present in this very moment, one can decide to change their lives completely. In this moment, one can make a powerful new decision. We have the power to create the reality we want in the present moment. The present moment is a magical place where your old-self dies and your new self is birthed constantly. It is a place of infinite possibilities and new realities that you can create. When you truly tap into this fact of the Universe, it is impossible not to fall in love with the present moment. The concept of time becomes irrelevant and the power of possibilities takes over. And as we surrender to the moment, we surrender to all the amazing possibilities being presented to us. We can come back to the moment by focusing on what is immediately around us. What do you see? What do you feel on your skin? What kind of scent are you present to? How does your body feel? When you want to come back to this present moment, come back to your senses and your body. Through this surrendering, we become lighter, we become closer to our creator-self, and we become powerful. We have the power to bring forth the future we desire starting right now.

And when we truly tap into this moment, we have the power to feel truly free. We become free from our past and from all the stories we carry heavily with us, and we experience freedom from the future that hasn't even happened yet. We become aligned and powerful knowing all the resources we need to create what we want right now already surround us. We get to come back to freedom and joy.

Exercise: Journaling

1. What is something in your life you have been worried about lately? What keeps you up at night?

____

____

____

2. Now look your answer from #1. Is this something you have control over? If no, write below "I choose to let go and come back to being present." If you do have control over it, write down 1 action step you can take today towards eliminating that worry.

____

____

____

3. If you chose to never sit in anxiety or fear again, as much as possible moving forward, what would become more possible for you?

____

____

____

4. Take a moment right now to practice mindfulness instead with space that opened up in your mind. What are some things that you notice around you? What do you see? What can you touch? What do you smell? What do you taste? What do you hear? How do you feel as you become more present with your current surroundings?

CHAPTER 17

DETACHING FROM THE ILLUSION OF "NORMAL"

Are you willing to die
from the illusion of reality
before you die
from your physical body?
Are you willing to
let go of the illusion of reality that
you and I are separate?
Are you willing to
see that a life without suffering
is not the same as
a life free of pain or pleasure,
but rather letting go of the resistance
from pain
and pleasure,
and all experiences in between?
And when you let go of the resistance,
what's left?
Who's left?
Who are you really?
Are you willing to be so courageous
to let that truth of you,
shine and lead the path?

What does your soul
authentically want to express
when you tune into that truth
of yours that shines so bright?
Can you be inspired,
not stay scared
of that Truth?

— y.c.

Free Yourself from the Societal Cage of "Normal"

What does it mean to you to be "normal"? Why did you choose to go to college, if you did? Why did you study for the SATs, if you did? Why did you get your first job, if you did? Do you know? I ask because these are things that I grew up thinking was the only way to be "normal" and I didn't even know why I never questioned my definition of normal for a while. I once met José, a seventeen-year-old who had already published twelve books about social media marketing and had his own agency. He lived in Puerto Rico and was already able to hack the internet business world—at seventeen!

When I was seventeen years old, I was in high school, studying for the SATs, trying to figure out which college to go to because I thought that was the only way to live life. I wasn't even thinking about what kind of impact I truly wanted to have in the world, or what I'd want to do with my college degree to fulfill my purpose in life. I didn't know I was supposed to discover my life purpose in high school or college. I didn't really know people my age could ever do anything, but I followed this prescribed path of college, job, and retire. Then after college, I got a corporate job. I didn't really know why—I just thought everyone did. It was what my parents told me would be best for me. I considered it "normal," especially from Korea where I am from. So I followed the norm because the thought that I could do something different didn't even cross my mind. Then I started seeing some friends taking very different routes from what I thought was possible. One friend was a videographer, creating amazing commercials and videos, and traveling the world; another was a YouTube influencer; another was a speaker and an author. The frequency of these stories showing up in my life from my closer connections started to increase, as if the Universe's message to me was getting louder and louder. Then one day, it hit me like a brick wall: I love writing, I love creating, and I love helping people to think of new possibilities. What am I doing at this corporate sales job where I am not doing any of those things that light up my soul? So then I decided to quit, and I decided to accept the Universe's invitation to step into my power.

Leaving the Normal Cage Offers Freedom

We always have the choice and the power to decide whether we want to follow our intuition or purpose versus chase the external ideals of being "normal." We have the power to create our own rules and free ourselves from any beliefs that keep us small and trapped. By owning that we are responsible for any decision in life, and that we have infinite power to create whatever path we desire, we start to feel empowered knowing we can truly achieve freedom from whatever we think is trying to keep us caged. It is up to us to let that happen or not. It is up to you to play bigger and outside of the cage of "normal." I choose freedom over and over again, over focusing on trying to fit into a societal cage now. This freedom offers me so much joy and adventure, and zest for life, knowing that I am creating my own reality.

Exercise

1. What are some beliefs that you consider "normal" that are inherited from your parents, family, or close friends?

____

____

____

____

2. What are some beliefs that you consider "normal" that you learned from your culture, ethnicity, or religion?

____

____

____

____

3. What are some beliefs that you consider "normal" that you adopted from your friends?

____

____

____

____

4. What are some beliefs that you consider "normal" that you adopted from the media?

___

___

___

___

5. If you gave yourself the permission slip not having to adhere to be "normal" according to these standards that you picked up from your life, what would you do that you've never done?

___

___

___

___

___

CHAPTER 18

FORGIVING & LETTING GO

today
I want to gift
myself
healing.
so
I forgive you.
— y.c.

Forgiveness is Unconditional Love

Chris Williams, on February 9, 2007, his worst nightmares came to life. He and his family were hit by a 17-year-old drunk driver, and his wife Michelle, who was pregnant with their 5th child, his son Benjamin, and his only daughter Anna passed away. He said he was having an out of body experience as he heard himself cry out loud as he saw his wife take her last breath. He said in that moment, he realized he only had one choice, and that was to forgive this young man. "The only thing I remember feeling and sensing is that I needed to let this go," said Williams in an interview. He learned that while he felt angry, he didn't have to direct it at another human. He decided to rely on his faith to God to guide him through the forgiving and grieving, trusting in an order larger than him. He didn't hesitate a moment with that decision to forgive this young man. What emerged for him was love and peace in his heart. He also gifted freedom for the 17-year-old and his family who would have otherwise drowned in guilt and shame. By him forgiving them, he got to grant them the true gift of love.

The Resistance Against Forgiving

Why should I forgive someone when they've hurt me? What's the key to forgiveness when there is lingering resentment inside? How do I even get started on forgiving someone? How do I forfeit my anger for someone, regardless of what they've done to me? What should I do to truly forgive?

"Resentment is like drinking poison and waiting for the other person to die."

This is an old saying. But recent research backs this up: long-lasting resentment due to lack of forgiving has negative effects on the non-forgiver's health. It becomes their own poison as they accept their position as a victim.

And we've all had situations where we've felt anger or resentment before. And *it's okay* to feel anger. It is never wrong (or right - it just is) to have any emotions. What we do with these emotions and how we allow them to manifest in our lives, though, can change the course of our lives. If Chris Williams decided to hold anger against the 17-year-old man, Chris's life, the 17-year-old's life, and his family's lives would all have been panned out differently.

And in this process, who Chris Williams really freed was, himself - freed himself from feeling anger and resentment, freeing himself to love more, freeing himself from lack of ease (dis-ease) in his own body from holding this anger. Anything repressed or avoided is bound to come out somehow. When you try to hold your resentment in, those unexpressed, hurt feelings can be triggered and come out in seemingly unrelated events, damaging the relationships that you care about the most. You choosing to direct that anger towards another person in the end hurts you more than anyone outside of you.

Hurt People Hurt People

Say that someone hurt you, because they were hurt, and it angered you. So then, you go out into the world with this ticking bomb inside you. Then because you hold so much resentment in your body and your heart, you find yourself being rude and mean to other people. Then the people you hurt go out there, and they hurt other people because of the anger that now *they* feel.

Can you see how continuing this cycle does not do you any good, the people around you any good, and most likely, the world any good? Can you see how if this cycle continues, there will just be more anger and hurt people in the world? Can you see now how healing yourself, and not reacting to that anger, but transforming that anger to the energy of love, like Chris Williams did, can eventually add to healing the world?

It has become an epidemic. Anger, resentment and hurting of other people can spread, when people aren't conscious enough of this cycle and give more energy to this cycle. So what if next time you feel wronged or hurt, you decide to stop the cycle. What if you, instead of reacting to the hurt person trying to hurt you, say to that person, "What can I do to help you suffer less?" Imagine if you can transmute fear and anger energy into love energy in that moment. Imagine if you can be a leader of love in that moment, instead of another helpless victim to fear. You get to consciously ask yourself: Do I wish to continue this cycle of resentment and anger in this world, or do I wish to show the power of love and compassion to end this cycle right here?

Letting Go of Being the Victim through Forgiveness

Often, when you haven't let go of the hurt inside and forgiven the other person, you might find yourself asking, "Why did this happen to me?" The quality of questions you ask can determine your quality of life. Asking "Why did this happen to me?" assumes you do not have the power to navigate powerfully through life. It assumes you're a victim and powerless. It assumes you want to reinforce the "why" behind this certain situation and justify that this is the type of experience you are inviting into your life. So rather, empower yourself in a situation that angers you by asking better questions, such as:

- "What can I learn from this experience?"
- "How lucky am I to be conscious enough to know that I have the power to stop this resentment cycle in this world?
- "How can I make sure I become the point where anger energy turns into love energy for the betterment of the world?"

See how much more empowering that is?

If you are having a hard time forgiving someone or a situation, go back to this question: How might this resentment be showing up in my own life in apparent and sneaky ways? Do I love myself enough to allow healing to happen by forgiving them? How would it feel to access and exercise my conscious choice to turn this point of anger and resentment into compassion, so that I single handedly stop this cycle of spreading more pain and suffering?

How would it feel to let go of this resentment? What new lessons merge for me as I forgive them? What can I do with the heart-space where resentment used to live to create instead the life I want? Would forgiving this person change who I am for better or worse?

So free yourself from resentment by forgiving them. Free yourself because forgiveness is really for your own freedom. And by forgiving, you clear more room in your heart for joy to emerge.

Story of Dana Liesegang of Forgiveness

There's also a story of my amazing friend Dana Liesegang. She is the author of the book *Falling Up: My Wild Ride from Victim to Kick-Ass Victory,* and I will never forget the story she told on stage about her story of forgiveness the first time I met her in Texas. She joined the Navy, being a strong adventurous soul even in her teens. When she was 19 years old, she was sexually assaulted and thrown off a cliff, left to face a battle with death. While she survived the fall, she was left paralyzed from her neck down. After a few years of living in despair, she decided to choose a different way of life, and that was one of believing in new possibilities through forgiveness. She decided to forgive the person who sexually assaulted her and almost killed her. What emerged for her was a new life of hope and love. She decided to write a book, start being vocal about her story of forgiveness and choosing love. The reward? Her freedom & inner peace.

I remember the first week into the quarantine in March of 2020 from the pandemic caused by covid-19, I called her to catch up and check in on her. "How are you doing during the quarantine?" I asked. After having gotten off a few calls that morning from people expressing their fears and frustrations, I was surprised to hear her upbeat, shiny voice that said "I am doing fantastic! I am so grateful for another day!" And I smiled, beaming back with love, remembering how powerful her mindset is and how powerful forgiveness has been for her.

Such amazing tales of forgiveness emerge in our society, not because terrible things don't happen. Instead, these people who choose to forgive, are choosing love; they are choosing spiritual freedom; they are choosing peace within; they are choosing their own right to be happy.

Exercise

1. Who do you get to forgive today for your own peace?

____

____

____

____

2. What is the positive intent behind your anger toward that person? Thank the anger for how it has served you. (Maybe it showed you that you are passionate about something, that your belief in something is very strong, what your boundaries are, or intense awareness around what you want to protect.)

____

____

____

____

3. What was stopping you from forgiving that person until now?

____

____

____

____

4. What would emerge for you if you were to forgive this person? Is it peace? Is it happiness? Is it love? Journal below.

____

____

____

____

For bonus points...

Reach out to the person in any medium accessible to you. If the person is not accessible anymore or you have a desire not to reach out, write the letter above to them that you don't send.

Ho'oponopono Prayer

I'd like to conclude this chapter with the healing Ho'oponopono prayer, which is a Hawaiian prayer for forgiveness. Saying this prayer for someone whom you feel entangled emotions for will allow you to release any unhealthy attachments and activate the healing process. Take a deep breath and put a loving intention on the person you would like to forgive. Then say this prayer out loud or silently, until your heart feels peace.

I love you.

I am sorry.

Please forgive me.

Thank you.

Part III

EXPANDING WITH THE UNIVERSE

CHAPTER 19

EMBODYING PLAYFULNESS & CURIOSITY

My inner child
in me
likes the inner child
in you.
Let's play.
— y.c.

Do you remember when you were a kid how you had no inhibition when trying to do a somersault, paint a new art piece with your bare hands, or build a sandcastle? Do you remember how when asked "what do you want to be when you grow up," you would name all the possibilities you dreamed about? Do you remember when you were little how you were happy, just because you could be? Do you ever wonder why when little kids meet other new kids, they go up to them fearlessly and hug them and call them their friend right away? Do you ever wonder how kids can be amused and excited over the smallest delights in life and laugh until they can't laugh any harder or anymore? When did we stop being playful, curious, and uninhibited?

"Be happy for no reason, like a child. If you are happy for a reason, you're in trouble, because that reason can be taken away from you."
— Deepak Chopra

Let this be a magnificent reminder that we don't need anything to be happy, when we are headed towards the journey of becoming our best selves. Operating from a place of curiosity and playfulness can bring about joy in creating new experiences with no fears. Being playful as an adult is about giving yourself the absolute and complete permission to be expressive about what your inner child wants. Play is one of the most powerful tools for getting creativity ignited, having fun, laughing, and being the light. Sometimes we become so serious about life as we "grow up." We dwell on what it means to be an adult, create social agreements around what is "normal" or "weird," and downplay our excitement when we meet someone we think is cool. What if we let that all go, and were led by our childlike curiosity and innate pull toward things that excite us?

Tuning in to Your Curiosity

Have you ever been curious about where curiosity comes from? Curiosity is a divine pull that guides you to an abundance of new experiences. How magical is this unexplainable pull that makes you want to uncover, explore, and experiment with something more! How amazing is this pull that creates new adventures, new questions, new connections, and sometimes new knowledge! Curiosity is the divine breadcrumb to guide you on your journey called life. Curiosity is the birthplace of new creations, ideas, inventions, and epiphanies. Curiosity is the igniting and sometimes pivoting point for new adventures.

Curiosity Ignites Creativity

Ed Catmull is the author of *Creativity, Inc.* and the President of Pixar. When Catmull was in school, no movies existed like the Pixar movies we know now. His curiosity about how computer graphics worked sparked all the creativity behind these movies we readily enjoy these days. In his book, Catmull talks about how in order to stay curious, one has to be without fear of being judged, like a child. Children are good at being expressive, and open, and curious; thereby accessing infinite creativity. Creativity is crucial for them because they are in the constant creative process of trying to make sense of the world around them through their pure set of lenses. However, when they start to get older, they become less creative and curious. As children get older and grow into being young adults or adults, they create a *fun blocker* and develop the fear of what others think or others judging them.

Adults, when did "explore, experiment" stop being your motto for life? What would happen if everyone approached the world with the curiosity of their inner child, and never let fear of failing, fear of being judged, or fear of looking stupid stop them from exploring and experimenting?

Curiosity is the Starting Point for All Adventures

As for me, after I quit my corporate job, for the first year when I committed to living following my curiosity, all of this unfolded:

- … got curious about painting and started painting for fun
    - Then I started selling my art online
    - Then I got invited to art shows and events where I was featured as a special guest artist
- … got curious about what it would be like to have my own yoga apparel line because yoga is one of my passions for life

    - So I started a yoga fit apparel line with a business partner
- ... got curious about what it would be like to hire a coach
    - So I hired one and shed a lot of my limiting beliefs that led me to so many incredible adventures
- ... got curious about what it would be like to do an open mic one day
    - I found places to perform at a few poetry open mics where I got to present my original poems which led to so much joy
- ... got curious what it would be like to explore Bali
    - So, I went to Bali and during my trip became inspired to write this book
- ... got curious about what it would be like to spread my message about happiness from a stage
    - So. I put my intention out there and manifested a speaking gig on stage!
- ... got curious about becoming an author
    - Here I am, and here you are reading this book!

So at this point, I hope you're wondering... "What miracles could unfold for me, if I trusted my curiosity as my divine guide towards joy and adventures?"

"Let yourself be silently drawn by the strange pull of what you really love. It will not lead you astray."

— Rumi

Exercise

1. What one thing can you do this week to help you access the feeling of being completely carefree like a child? (Dance in your room, sing carefree in your shower, hug someone you love with pure joy in your heart, etc.)

____

____

____

2. If you were to notice something in your room through the eyes of a child today, what would you find amazing or be curious about that you didn't notice before?

____

____

____

3. What are some wonders of the world you don't have answers to?

____

____

____

CHAPTER 20

EMBRACING YOUR FAILURES

life is about
trial and error.
trial is your courage to life;
error is your surrender
to your imperfections
as a human being. Between
the colorful cycles of
courage and surrender,
we live, we love, we hurt,
and we learn.
and that is life.
and I wouldn't have it
any other way.
— y.c.

Have you ever failed in your life? Towards the journey of creating happiness and on the way to your best self, if you haven't failed, you haven't pushed yourself outside of your comfort zone. So if you've failed, congratulations! You're human, enjoying the full experience of growth and expansion!

Guess Who Else Has Failed? Every winner. Every human.

Elon Musk is a billionaire visionary and the CEO of many companies, including Tesla, Hyperloop, SpaceX, and the Boring Company. But can I remind you that he had to blow up a few rockets before he had a successful launch? Can I inform you, if you don't already know, that he had to be fired from his own CEO position from his own company before he learned to be a better leader and manager? Did you know that he was once labeled a maniac boss during his days at PayPal because of his sense of perfectionism that drove a lot of people crazy? But what's magnificent about Elon Musk is that those "failures" didn't stop him from doing what he loves to do. "If something is important enough, you should try, even if the probable outcome is failure," Musk says.

J. K Rowling, the international author of the *Harry Potter* series is also known for her difficult days of getting rejected by many publishers and being on welfare while she wrote her billion-dollar story, before she became *the* J. K. Rowling. When Thomas Edison was once asked about his thousands of failed attempts to invent a lightbulb, his answer was that he hadn't failed! He had only found a thousand ways not to make a lightbulb.

When you start to experiment with participating in new activities, meeting new people, going to new places, trying new challenges, and so on, as you start to live with your life with more untamed curiosity, you will initially inevitably experience some that feel like failures. No one is perfect or can make perfect decisions all the time especially in the beginning of trying something new. But if you let the fear of those failures stop you from trying altogether, you would miss out on all the adventures and memories.

As you can see, successful people aren't people who never failed; they are people who failed, failed, and failed so many times, and kept going anyway *despite* their many failures. In fact, they see it as part of their natural journey and progression toward their ultimate success. When people can view "failures" as stepping stones toward success, they can find motivation, drive, and flow even in their season of what seems like failures. They know that making mistakes and failed attempts mean that they are on the right track to their vision.

So can you give yourself permission to fail, so that you do not live a life ignoring your unique gifts? Can you give yourself the permission to shine so that our world doesn't miss out on your magic? Imagine if Edison quit after the first 500 times that he tried to make the lightbulb and how different our lives would be right now. The Universe needs *you* to step in with your gifts in this co-creation and co-expanding process. Ignoring your own gifts due to fear of failure does not serve our Universe at the highest level. Your unique gifts *will* shine, if you persist until you make sure it does. Have faith. Keep going.

Failing is a Gift in Disguise

Sharon Lechter is one of those women that's hard to imagine that she's had many failures at a glance. It seems as if she turns everything into gold. She is the co-author of *Rich Dad, Poor Dad,* Co-Founder of the Rich Dad Company, home of the CASHFLOW game, the official annotator for *Outwitting the Devil,* co-author of *Three Feet from Gold,* author of *Think and Grow Rich for Women,* and appointed to the

President's Council for Financial Literacy for both Presidents Bush & Obama administrations. And these are just a very small tip of the iceberg for what she's achieved and created in her life. At the *Global Virtual Summit,* I got the honor to interview her. Although I know deep down everyone experiences failures, does someone like Sharon Lechter also experience big failures? "I am curious, Sharon. Does a powerful businesswoman like you have any notable failures in your past?" I asked. And she told me that rather early in her career, she made a *very* bad business decision. "It was just a complete failure from a business standpoint." She paused then continued,

"... but Yuri, because of that business, I ended up in a room in a meeting that I wouldn't have been at otherwise," she said, "and that's when I met this handsome man, Michael." I smiled, noticing that when she talked about this special man, she lit up like a teenager in love. "And Michael is my husband of over 40 years, and the love of my life. And he's been the *biggest* blessing of my life. So truly, there are no failed experiences. Napoleon Hill said, "Out of every failure comes the seed of equal or greater benefit. There's hidden gifts in every failure."

Being Playful about your Failures

So as Sharon talks about, failure is truly just a different word for a "hidden gift." Creating a playful, forgiving, and experimental attitude toward the idea of potential failure can empower you to continue to move forward, instead of freezing in fear. So try this on: letting go of the need *always* win and releasing the unrealistic expectation to avoid 100% of your failures. In fact, get excited for the next failure because there might be unexpected blessings hidden in those that may catapult you forward, and why those had to happen along your journey will only make sense to you later on. Trust the divine process. Sharon's life, and most people's lives expand because of failures, and not the opposite when we allow room for the lessons and blessings to surface. And when you can internalize that you get to expand even through your failures, you become even more fearless to live and create the reality that truly fulfills you.

Exercise

1. What are some failures you have experienced in the past?

____

____

____

2. How did these experiences affect you? What were the hidden gifts or lessons in those failures, looking back?

____

____

____

____

____

____

____

CHAPTER 21

EXPANDING THROUGH RESILIENCE

I almost caught a
bullet with my mouth.
I almost tasted the metallic
bitter traces of death
that melted on my tongue.
people say I almost died
that day.
here's the secret:
that's the day I started living.
— y.c.

Does life feel difficult at times? Does life feel confusing? Does it sometimes feel like an uphill battle and you feel mentally and physically exhausted? I get it. I, too, have had moments like that; It sometimes feels like you are barely surviving, and moment by moment, you are uncertain whether you will make it. You are terrified that you don't see the light at the end of the tunnel, yet. You start to think, *Why me?* You want to just call it quits sometimes. Life is exhausting, you say to yourself internally. Then you lose hope. Then you get depressed. Then you doubt your own abilities or God. You wonder if the Universe is really taking care of you. You lose faith

Thriving on Your Journey

What adversities have you faced in your life? How did you respond to them or overcome them? What did you learn from overcoming them? Have you let go of any resentment or anger around this adversity, if there was any? What are you going through right now? How do you see yourself becoming more powerful once you overcome your current adversity that you're going through, if any? What if those adversities help you find your superpowers? And what if you get to know in your heart that you expand as a soul, a human being, and a positive light to the world through those challenges that you have faced, or are currently facing? What if in the end, adversities lead us to live a life of fulfillment and joy even more?

Shifting from Survive to Thrive

"I didn't survive. I prepared." This is what Nelson Mandela said in an interview with Tony Robbins, when he was asked how he was able to "survive" being wrongfully incarcerated for twenty-seven years. He was a leader in advocating for human rights and equality for all people of South Africa. During his time locked away, he missed a quarter of his life; he had every "right" to be depressed, resentful, or angry—he even missed his mother and eldest son's funerals while in prison. But instead of harboring anger toward the people who took away his freedom, he "prepared" to forgive them during those twenty-seven years and "prepared" to move forward with the impact he wanted to create for humanity. In his mind, it wasn't the people who put him there, because he believed that people are good. But he saw this as a breakdown in the system, and so he was determined to change the system when he got out.

He unconditionally loved all the people of his nation. He saw the oppression and adversity he witnessed in his country as an opportunity to build the nation's strength and resiliency, rather than a reason to stay focused on his anger.

Mandela led with love, not fear. He saw this time as a period of hope, not darkness. He saw it as a time to build character, not a time of self-destruction. He never gave up on his dream to bring equality and freedom back to South Africa and all its people. His physical body was jailed, but his spirit soared more and more every day. That is why when Mandela got out, he wasn't looking for revenge, drowning in resentment or playing victim. He wasn't focused for twenty-seven years simply on "surviving." He was "preparing" to change the world for the better. And he knew the most powerful way to achieve the outcome he wanted was to stay true to his intention of spreading true love for all people. Nelson Mandela was able to expand his influence and powerfully share his message of love and equality due to his preparation during the time of false incarceration. In 1993, he won the Nobel Peace Prize for the peaceful end he brought to apartheid. And, at age seventy-five, he was elected as the first non-white president of South Africa. Mandela was able to live a powerful, fulfilling life, even through his adversities. His commitment to move forward towards his vision and his drive to thrive was greater than any adversity he faced.

A Note on Resilience

Experiences come in seasons. Your life ebbs and flows. And all of our experiences are temporary and help us grow. And especially challenges in our lives make us more resilient. Andrew Solomon is one of my favorite human activists and storytellers and I love his message on resilience. In his Ted Talk, *How the Worst Moments in Our Lives Define Who We Are,* which has over 6.5 million views last time I checked, he talks about how difficult moments help us construct our identity. As a gay man growing up in America, he faced discrimination for many of his younger years. He talks about how even though looking back, those times were hard, it allowed him to create meaning for his life and create the foundation for his character. In that journey of facing adversities and finding out what he's made of, he was able to become more resilient, allowing him to become the award-winning author and humanitarian he is today, impacting millions of people with his message.

Practical Guidelines to turn Adversities to Confidence

Imagine that adversities we face are like big boulders in our paths towards our best selves. They throw you off for a second and you can't seem to see what's a few inches ahead of you because of this giant boulder that is 10x bigger than you. So these are the steps you can take:

1. **Clarity of the Situation**: You take a moment to take in your new surrounding and new situation without judgement. You get to examine the size of this adversity (boulder) at hand. You get clarity on what is going on.

2. **Recalibration:** You recalibrate as fast as you can and realize you have a choice about what to do with this big rock in your path. You remember that running into an obstacle in life isn't unique to you or mankind, and that you will get through this.

3. **Commitment to Overcome:** Choose to thrive. You intentionally decide you will get through this. In fact, you decide that not only will you get through this, but you will appreciate every step of the journey, and proudly share this story one day. This gets to be your story of how you became stronger, more powerful, and resilient.

4. **Gratitude:** You forgive and appreciate. It is no one's fault that this is happening. This is the divine gift for you to grow. This is happening *for* you. So you even start to appreciate all the people, factors, and situations that got you here because now you get to build character. You start to notice the good things in your new situation, despite its challenges. You find the beauty even of the boulder itself.

5. **Connecting to Source:** You take this time to connect with God, the Universe, or your highest self, and you feel hopeful and comforted knowing this is the journey that will lead to your greatness. You ask for guidance: Source, you created this rock and you created me. Knowing that all things in the Universe is here to conspire towards my best self, what can I learn here?

6. **Re-establishing trust in yourself, others, and Universe:** In this place, you start to lead with love, for yourself, for your character-building process, for your enemies, for the inevitable factors that got you there, for God, and/or for the Universe. You start to feel amazing knowing you can find love and light even in dark times, and you gain another level of respect for yourself.

7. **Take action:** You then take action to conquer climbing this boulder ahead of you and continue on your path. You thrive through your adversity!
8. **Confidence & Expansion:** You feel your spirit expanding to a capacity you never reached before. You start to ask yourself, if I can climb and conquer that huge boulder, what else can I do in life that I didn't think was possible at a glance?

And when you get to know who you are deeply, through these adversities, you get to create deep appreciation for self and fulfillment for your life knowing what you're truly made of.

Note: Don't Ever Give Up and Surrender to Gratitude

So the message from your inner resilience for you is this: whatever you're going through right now, don't ever give up. If you are going through a difficult time now, I invite you to let go of resentment and the idea that you have to survive through whatever you are going through. Rather, use your difficult time as fuel to expand and thrive towards the best version of yourself and a life of joy leading with love. And that love can start with love for yourself, love for other people, and expanding all the way to the love for a cause bigger than you. This process allows you to expand with the difficult waves of life, instead of contracting and becoming small and resentful. And you weren't created by the Universe to be small. You are a miracle of infinite possibilities with joy and fulfillment as your birthright! So play big by using your hardships as a springboard to the next version of yourself. It gives you an opportunity to empower yourself and others to create a big bang and a ripple effect of positive influence around the globe. Remember, you are a creator, with all the power to create and expand with the Universe.

Exercise

1. Reflect back on a time when you felt like giving up, but didn't and kept going. Journal about what you were going through, what fears or obstacles were present that led you to almost giving up, and what inspired you to keep going.

____

____

____

2. What was the outcome of this situation and what did you learn about yourself?

____

____

____

3. Now read this story and the lesson as if it were not your own. Scan the people in your life. What positive traits would you acknowledge about this person in this story? Who could benefit from hearing this story?

____

____

____

4. Share this story to one other person in the next twenty-four hours. (If you have social media, you can post it there, too.) Write down who you

share this to and journal about your experience here. If this feels out of your comfort zone to you at first, you can start by saying, "Hey when is a good time to chat? I'd love to connect deeper with you and share something that I've never shared before." Let the magic and healing unfold.

____

____

____

____

____

CHAPTER 22

CREATING ABUNDANCE THROUGH COURAGE

courage is

the magic wand of

an alchemist.

courage

transmutes

fear

into

creation.

— y.c.

Courage: From Fear to Creative Energy

Have you ever hidden behind your fears? Have you ever hidden your fears away from everyone so no one can see them? Have you ever felt like showing your fears would make you look weak? Hey infinite beings, can you do this for yourself, and for the rest of the Universe? Will you share your fears with us, so we can see all of you? So, you can give your fears a chance to transform into creative energy?

Express your fears Intentionally

Becoming aware and expressing your fears lessens their power over you. This chapter might feel counterintuitive at first. Why would I want to express my fears out loud? Doesn't that give it more energy? It depends on the intention. Often, when people just complain about their fears, their intention is to feel validated *for* having those fears. Their intention isn't to shift out of those fears. Their intention isn't to be in full acceptance of yourself, even with those fears.

And here is the thing: Fear kept hidden in your mind can appear way more powerful than it actually is in reality. Oftentimes, your fears can be very irrational and purely the result of your mind's imagination. And when you keep your fears to yourself, and try to hide them away, you don't get to actually grow out of your fears.

And if your intention is to shift out of your fears, when you hide them away, no one can offer you resources to help you, even if they have them. And your fears are also a part of you. No one can see you for who you really are, if you hide the parts of you with fears. In that, you practice selective self-acceptance and self-love, rather than complete, unconditional self-acceptance and self-love. If you express your fears with the intention of shifting out of them and turning them into a creative, resourceful state, then something magical happens: your fears' powers diminish in sharing them to others. The fears no longer consume you or have any power over you. They no longer live inside your body or try to manifest through uncontrolled ways, such as outburst of anger or anxiety. This trapped energy of fear can become negative, draining energy for your body.

In these moments, I want to remind you of a magical energy called courage. Courage is the catalyst that transmutes fear into new possibilities. Courage carries the energy of both fear and new possibilities. This is why when one accesses courage, you are both scared and excited at the same time. Through courage, you can start to expand, shifting fear energy into creative energy.

Fear to Courage Alchemy, A Self-Leadership Technique: How to Shift Fear into New Possibilities through Courage

Here I offer a technique to express your fears, so they lose their power, leaving you more creative and abundant.

1. Identify your fear for what it is. Write out exactly what you are scared of. For example, if you have a fear of public speaking, write out fully what fears come up around that. Write out this fear of yours starting with this statement, "A part of me feels fear about..." to acknowledge that it is not your entire and every part of your body, mind and soul that feels fear. There is only a part of you that is present to this fear. (For example: A part of me feels fear about speaking tomorrow in front of people).

A part of me feels fear about ...

____

____

____

____

2. Follow up this fear statement with this statement, "I have created a story in my mind" to see what stories you have created around that fear. (For example: *I have created a story in my mind* that people will make fun of me or judge me.)

I have created a story in my mind ...

____

____

____

3. Now, take a moment to honor the part of you that creates a vision based on fear. What was the positive intent behind this fear, knowing that every emotion has a purpose? What was it trying to protect you from? What can you appreciate about this fear? Write this out with this statement, "I am grateful to recognize the positive intent of my fear that was trying to…." Then follow up this statement with "I realize now that my imagined fear does not actually threaten my physical well-being which is what the fear was thinking it was doing. I choose to focus on the amazing and likely possibility I am creating instead, knowing that even if my fear manifests, it doesn't mean anything about me. (For example: I am grateful to recognize the positive intent of my past fear that was trying to protect me from the imagined social threat of being made fun of or being judged. I realize being made fun of or being judged does not actually threaten my physical well-being. I choose to focus on the amazing and likely possibility I am creating instead, knowing that even if my fear manifests, it doesn't mean anything about me.)

I am grateful to recognize the positive intent of my fear that was trying to…

____

I realize now that my imagined fear that was trying to…

____

I choose to focus on the amazing and likely possibility I am creating instead, knowing that even if my fear manifests, it doesn't mean anything about me.

4. Now knowing what the fear was trying to do for you, we get to release it and turn the page, so it is in the past. Change the story from Step 1 to past tense, then add the statement "until now." (For example: A part of me used to feel fear about speaking tomorrow in front of people. I had created a story in my mind that people will make fun of me or judge me, *until now.*)

A part of me used to feel fear about...

____

____

____

I had created a story in my mind...

____

____

____

until now.

5. At this point create a vision of what you truly want to create in the given situation, when your initial fear is absent. This is the process of accessing courage to turn fear into a creative state. You get to identify the choices you can create regarding your situation that used to be consumed with fear. You can decide if that is a story you want to stay with or move past in this moment through your energy of courage. Write out what your new vision could look like, by starting with "A part of me

feels inspired about…" and adding a "because I have created a possibility in my mind…" statement to follow up that has a flair of gratitude and the benefits that you can bring to the world by overcoming your own fears (For example: A part of me now feels inspired about speaking in front of people tomorrow because I have created a possibility in my mind that people will benefit and appreciate the unique story I am blessed to tell.")

A part of me now feels inspired about…

____

____

____

____

…because I have created a possibility in my mind…

____

____

____

6. Now combine all and write it out below. Take a deep breath, and read out loud, connecting to your courage and creative energy. Focus powerfully on the new story you created while acknowledging and appreciating the positive intent of this fear. (For example: *A part of me feels fear about* speaking tomorrow in front of people. *I have created a story in my mind* that people will make fun of me or judge me. I am grateful to recognize the positive intent of my fear that was trying to protect me from the imagined social threat of being made fun of or being judged. I realize being made fun of or being judged does not actually

threaten my physical wellbeing. I choose to focus on the amazing and likely possibility I am creating instead, knowing that even if my fear manifests, it doesn't mean anything about me. A part of me used to feel fear about speaking tomorrow in front of people because I had created a story in my mind that people will make fun of me or judge me, *until now*. A part of me now feels inspired about speaking in front of people tomorrow because I have created a possibility in my mind that people will benefit and appreciate the unique story I am blessed to tell.)

Now your turn to put it all together:

A part of me feels fear about...

____

I have created a story in my mind...

____

I am grateful to recognize the positive intent of my fear...

____

I realize now that my imagined fear that was trying to…

____

I choose to focus on the amazing and likely possibility I am creating instead, knowing that even if my fear manifests, it doesn't mean anything about me.

A part of me used to feel fear about....

____

… I have created a story in my mind…..

____

... until now.

A part of me now feels inspired about...

____

... because I have created a possibility in my mind...

____

Try this exercise to see how it feels for a fear that is present to you today. Feel yourself as you shift fear out of your body and lead yourself to fully express and recognize, appreciate, and then release and transmute your fear into a new creative possibility through courage. And it is in this natural state of creativity that humans can truly be peaceful, joyful and be happy.

Exercise: Journaling

1. What are some fears that are present to you in your own life today?

____

____

____

2. Use the format from the **Fear to Courage Alchemy: Self Leadership Technique** above to shift these fears out of your body into new possibilities below for additional fears that were identified below.

A part of me feels fear about

____

I have created a story in my mind

____

I am grateful to recognize the positive intent of my fear

I realize now that my imagined fear that was trying to…

I choose to focus on the amazing and likely possibility I am creating instead, knowing that even if my fear manifests, it doesn't mean anything about me.

A part of me used to feel fear about...

… I have created a story in my mind…

… until now.

A part of me now feels inspired about…

… because I have created a possibility in my mind…

Part IV

EXPRESSION

Chapter 23

Leveraging your emotions

Here's the thing.
everything is made of love.
Everything.
Every emotion is a shade of love.
The opposite of love,
isn't fear.
Fear is a shade of love,
for if you didn't love something,
you wouldn't fear losing it.
The opposite of love,
isn't anger.
Anger is a shade of love
for if you didn't love,
you wouldn't get angry enough to protect it.
The opposite of love
isn't disappointment.
Disappointment is a shade of love,
for if you didn't love,
you wouldn't put an exciting expectation on it.
The opposite of love
isn't jealousy or envy,
for if you didn't love,
you wouldn't envy enough to want what they have.

The opposite of love
isn't hatred,
for if you didn't love,
we wouldn't hate how far
we've strayed away from our true potential,
our true ideals of love.
The only true opposite of love,
is lack of participation
In this Universe
because
when you're not here,
when you block out these shades of love,
and you disconnect and hide,
then we can't see you,
we can't experience any colors of love,
any colors of you.
So come play,
in this playground,
where all emotions are welcomed
and you're allowed to get messy.
And here, all expressions of you,
are celebrated, because
you can't fool us, even if you tried,
all colors of emotions
are just reincarnations of love.
So don't be afraid,
I see you.
When you fearlessly paint the world with

all different shades of love,
that's how I know,
you're a child of God;
Your love is abundant in all your expressions
of who you are.
So be here,
Be with us.
when we color together,
when we get messy together,
we are just painting this canvas,
this Universe,
with more
love.
— y.c.

Understanding the Different Spectrum of Emotions

Let's expand on emotions for a moment. How do we define emotions? What is an emotion? What is our relationship to our emotions? Do we suppress or do we express our emotions? Do we react with an emotion or create an emotion? What are the benefits and consequences of doing either?

The question, "What is an emotion?" will never have one simple answer. There is no scientific consensus when it comes to knowing how to define what an emotion is simply. What we may consider about emotions is that:

1. Emotions are your internal guide to you and teach you about yourself.
2. Emotions are all variations of love (refer to the poem above). They all show us about love in different ways.
3. Emotion is energy in motion, and each emotion vibrates at a different level. Some emotions make us vibrate slower, and some vibrate faster.

When emotions are fully expressed, they are what make us feel most human and alive. When we feel stuck, it's often because we haven't fully expressed all emotions fully. Yet, isn't it true that in our society being *too emotional* comes with a certain flavor of stigma and judgement? Isn't it true that showing emotions is often associated with being weak? And so, we suppress them. We suppress, instead of expressing, our emotions. Rather than being in the experience of each emotion, and allowing them to flow through us, we suppress the emotions and all the lessons and wisdom that could have come from them. In this suppression, we feel stuck. We become energetically constipated. We have created a world where many will do anything to numb out these emotions, rather than allowing these emotions to flow through. When emotions flow through us, we experience these emotions, then let them go. They don't get stuck in our bodies. So we become light and free. Freedom is in allowing these emotions to surface and be expressed. Freedom is knowing that these emotions come and go, like a guest; they are never permanent.

Empower Yourself by Understanding these Concepts about Emotions

Here are some things you get to know about you and your emotions to empower and free yourself, even more:

1. *You* are the creator of your emotions. You are the individual who feels and responsible for all your emotions. You are in charge of creating any emotions. No one can create or take away an emotion for you. No one can *make* you feel a certain way. You allow it. You are in control. You have the power.
2. All your emotions are valid, real, and deserve to exist. You don't have to judge them.
3. … But *you* are not your emotions. Remember, you are the creator of your emotions.
4. Emotions are not permanent, and they are being created each moment. Each emotion can be birthed and can die each new moment. Therefore, the creator and the experiencer of the emotions, you, can choose to stay in a certain emotional state for however long as you want. You can choose into another emotion after you've learned the lessons and the wisdom it offers, if you choose to.
5. Emotions are expressions of your soul; each emotion has a positive intent (or the light side) and a shadow side. No emotions are good, bad, right or wrong.

6. Emotions can be fully processed and released, when you can internalize both the emotion's positive intent (purpose, benefit) and its shadow.
7. Emotion resonates with a certain vibrational frequency of energy and attracts more of the same energy (which is what we explored in the last chapter). Therefore, as you claim your power back to manage your emotional state, you become an even more powerful manifestor to attract the types of experiences you truly desire.

Taking Back Power for Your Emotions

So how do you take your power back when it comes to your emotions? Most people aren't trained on *what* to do with their emotions when they surface. A lot of people give their power away by not taking ownership of their own emotions. Some people blame the external world, people, and other things outside of themselves for the emotions that *they* generated as a reaction to the external world. Often, we forget that emotions are purely how *we* react to our own experience, and no one else's. No one can technically *make* you feel a certain emotion. I've heard my client once say in our initial sessions, when talking about a conflict with another, something like, "Oh, they *made* me so angry when they ______." How could someone *make* you feel an emotion when you are the person who created that emotion from within you? How could someone *make* you feel angry when you are the one reacting to a certain situation? Have you ever been in a situation where you had completely different emotions than someone else in response to the same event or same person's behavior? If people can respond differently to the same thing, then is it really the person or external situation that created that emotion *within* you?

And so we say things such as:

"You make me so angry!"

"You make me happy!"

"She is the only thing that makes me happy in my life"

"He makes me feel bad about myself."

Consciously or subconsciously, when we say they *made* us feel a certain way, we are denying that we are the creator of our own emotions. We are forgetting for a minute that we are choosing to react with that particular emotion based on what the other person did. That's why one person can say the same thing to different people, and they can have two completely different responses.

Person A: "Your hair looks nice today!"

Person B: "Aw thank you!" [emoting joy and gratitude]

or ...

Person A: "Your hair looks nice today!"

Person C: "Are you mocking me? I am having a bad hair day." [emoting shame/unworthiness]

So when we choose into an emotion or a reaction, recognize that it is one of the infinite ways that we can feel in that moment. None of these responses are right or wrong; and every emotion is valid. Each emotion shows us what we get to celebrate, what we get to heal, what we get to let go of or what we get to create.

Freeing yourself from fear-based emotions

Let us now explore the different emotions in a little bit more in detail. While staying away from categorizing emotions as good or bad, it might be more beneficial to categorize them as either fear/scarcity-oriented or creative/growth-oriented emotions. This allows us to understand the underlying energy behind these emotions. This section explores emotions that fall under the fear & scarcity-oriented emotions, such as, well starting with fear, anger, depression, grief and shame.

Fear

Positive intent of fear:

- Fear's number one goal is to protect you.
- Fear shows you your ability to urgently reallocate resources to protect yourself (like running away with all your strength if there is a tiger chasing you).
- Fear shows you where the edges of your limiting beliefs are, so that you can breakthrough them (if the fear is arising from a situation that doesn't actually threaten the physical safety of the body, such as public speaking)

Shadows of fear:

- Fear can be completely irrational, unless the fear is related to protecting your physical safety.
- Fear can stop you from moving forward, if you freeze due to fear.

- Fear can ignite reaction, if you go into fight or flight mode, which can lead to destructive outcome or takes you further away from your vision
- Fear and stress, when chronic, can destroy the health of your mental state and the health of your physical body

Fear arises when our bodies go into fight or flight mode because it senses a threat. Fear can serve as a protector from potentially dangerous situations. The problem with fear is that we often feel it in situations that do not actually threaten our physical well-being. Us, humans, can sometimes see social situations that threaten our ego as equally threatening as a threat to our physical safety, which is not true. Although exceptions exist, most social situations do not threaten an individual's actual survival. For instance, if public speaking scares you, what you're actually scared of is the potential social rejection or lack of acceptance from your peers; it has nothing to do with the safety of your physical body (public speaking won't *kill* you, for the most part).

When fear inappropriately steps in where immediate physical danger doesn't exist, it can actually create a more negative than positive consequence because it tries to protect you from things you don't need *actual* protection from. You do not need to hide from your audience when you are giving your speech; they are not trying to physically harm you or put you in danger. But it is the thought that they might do something to hurt your ego, that makes the irrational fear come up.

Fear's original intent to serve your well-being is loving because it wants to protect you and help you to get through a difficult situation. For example, in high school, my friend was in the car that her brother was driving on New Year's Eve and almost got hit by a drunk driver swerving. Immense fear kicked in for her brother, causing him to swerve their car effectively just in time to miss the car coming at them. Through fear and the increased level of cortisol it can activate, we can sometimes access superhuman powers hiding within us to help us and get out of a difficult situation.

But what do we do when irrational fears try to overwhelm us when our physical well-being is not threatened? We can allow ourselves to thank our fears for the positive reason it exists in our bodies. Its positive intent is to protect us and so we get to acknowledge the intention of it existing. Then we get to release the fear because it does not serve us in that situation no longer after the original intent is realized. Then we can lead our bodies into a state of calmness through meditation or breathing exercise as outlined below. That calmness allows us to access a blank canvas of emotions so we can then powerfully choose into another emotion that we'd rather create and feel in that moment, such as gratitude.

Exercise for When You Feel Fear

One way to release fear is by calming our bodies and mind through a breathing exercise. Here is the process:

1. Sit in a comfortable position, crossing your legs and keeping your spine straight.
2. Close your eyes.
3. With your right hand, place your index and middle finger between your eyebrows.

4. To facilitate breathing through your nostril to relax your body, gently place your ring finger on your left nostril as you inhale through your right nostril for four counts.
5. Hold your breath at the top for another four counts.
6. Exhale slowly out of your left nostril as you press down gently on your right nostril with your thumb for four counts.
7. Hold at the bottom of your exhale for four breaths.
8. Repeat this process for seven to ten breaths.
9. Reverse the circular breathing by closing your right nostril first to inhale for four counts. Then hold for four counts. Then exhale through your left nostril.
10. Repeat for the same amount of time you did on the other side.
11. When finished, open your eyes, and notice and appreciate your relaxed and present mind.

Anger

Let's talk about anger. We've all felt this fire energy before. Before we begin, spend a moment to recall a time when you felt really angry and the reasons behind that anger.

Positive Intent of Anger:

- Anger shows us what is *really* important to us and what we want to protect.
- Anger can ignite courage.
- Anger can inspire massive action.

- Anger can protect boundaries.
- Anger can empower you out of feeling like a victim.
- Anger can alert us when there is a perceived danger.
- Anger can temporarily make you move fast and be strong.

Shadows of Anger:

- Anger keeps you in scarcity/survival mode.
- Anger limits your ability to be creative.
- Anger will cause suffering.
- Anger is destructive.
- Anger limits your spiritual growth.
- Anger is an emotion from the past.
- Anger limits your ability to create a win-win.
- Anger can cause a person to act as if they are intoxicated.
- Anger can cause violence.

When anger arises within us, it shows us what's important to us. It shows us what we value so much in life that we want to protect it actively. Remember the movie *Taken*? In the movie, the retired CIA agent's daughter is kidnapped in a foreign country by a sex trafficking ring. The dad, fuming with anger, will do anything, including risking his own life and killing others, to protect what's very important to him, his daughter.

Anger can also be dangerous because when we are angry, it is easy not to see the positive intent of why the other person is doing what they're doing, or what your anger is showing *ourselves* about *our own selves*. Anger, much like fear, is a stress-hormone activated response. To better manage anger over time, it is crucial to create a better emotional climate overall by going back to the basics. Going back to the basics could include habits that reduce my body's stress-hormone levels, such as creating a less stressful environment, sleeping enough, exercising regularly, reducing substances that induce stress in the body such as alcohol, and meditating every day.

Also, with mindfulness practice over time, we can develop awareness around our anger. We can start to become the master of our anger, rather than stay the slave of it. This mindfulness practice could look like what I highlight step-by-step below.

One helpful thing to remember is that anger is also energy related to love. Anger shows us our amplified fear of losing something or someone we love and our desire to protect something that is really important to us. When we remember that anger is also energy related to love, we are reminded that we can also learn to acknowledge anger for what it truly shows us. And when we can acknowledge anger, release it, then transmute that intense energy into creative energy, it can be extremely powerful.

In a nutshell, here are the steps for releasing anger and transforming it to creative energy:

1. Acknowledge anger. Give yourself a set amount of time to be angry and commit to feeling it fully. Go scream in a pillow. Go

for a run. Go cry. Move the energy around. Set a timer for 10 minutes, 30 minutes, whatever you need to fully be in the experience of anger real time. Important thing here is not to direct this anger at anyone, including you.

2. Honor the positive intent of anger. Ask yourself: What is it showing me that's important? What do I feel strongly about?
3. Thank the anger for showing you what's important to you.
4. Release it: Visualize where anger is in your body and visualize breathing it out. Come back to calmness.
5. Now consciously and powerfully choose an emotional state that better serves you. Can you be grateful that your anger taught you something, if anything?
6. From this place, think about what you can create and can add to the world from what your anger taught you. (i.e. When I realized that I was angry at the world after someone close to me attempted suicide, it taught me how important it was for me that people get to talk about what they're really going through instead of trying to mask it. I eventually released that anger by thanking it for showing me what's really important to me, which was to eliminate stigma and increase awareness around mental health so that people can get help openly and earlier if they feel that they need help. Then I got to come back to feeling inspired about what I can do to start changing the world regarding the stigma and awareness around mental health. I ended up joining American Foundation for Suicide Prevention as a volunteer

where I gave time, money and energy to contribute back to this cause. I am thankful for the anger that showed me this because it allowed me to learn what I care about and it showed me how I can contribute back to society. This is an example of turning anger into creative energy.)

Depression

Positive intent of depression:

- Depression is reminding you that your soul is asking you to slow down and heal.
- Depression shows you your need for extra self-care.
- Depression shows you your additional need for connection.
- Depression shows you your unprocessed, suppressed emotions and experiences need to be released.

Shadows of depression:

- Depression slows down your vibration.
- Depression can lead to feeling sick, stuck or unproductive.
- Depression can become lethal if healing and self-care are not honored properly.
- Depression leaks energy, so people feel "drained." Depression cuts off flow of life.
- Depression lacks passion and gratitude for life.

One reason it is so important to address and never suppress an emotion like depression is because an emotion can get trapped in your body. This can cause harm to your body and soul if not properly surfaced and expressed. Staying in a fear-based emotion, such as depression, for too long without consciously coming out of it can block the authentic "flow" of human experience and become destructive. So instead of trying to fight off any emotions or avoid them, it is helpful to become present with whatever you are feeling, and allow your body to channel through the emotion, rather than become a stubborn storage of it. So when depression is present, acknowledge it as a sign to focus on self-care, to pour into and fill your own cup first, and to make that a priority. This way, depressed emotion gets processed and released, rather than getting stuck.

Prayer for Self-Love

Put your hands on your heart. Bless yourself with these words.

I call upon the Infinitely Loving Universe to bless my body, my soul and my heart today, in this moment. I invite unconditional love to every cell in my body, every bone, every fiber of my muscles, and every part of my being. I bless my body as I am deeply grateful for this vessel for my soul, as it allows me to honor my soul's wishes everyday. I am grateful for my body as it allows me to move, allows me to eat, allows me to breathe, allows me to do all the things that my soul desires, and allows me to live this gift called life. I am grateful for my soul as it sources infinite wisdom for every next step in my life. When I get calm and quiet, I am blessed to be able to hear my soul's guide clearly and loudly. I am grateful for my heart, as it generates loving intentions out for the universe to expand and it beats everyday to allow me to live a meaningful life. I am thankful for myself and I am blessed to receive unconditional love from the universe today, in this moment and always.

Grief

Positive intent of grief:

- Shows you you have healing to do
- Shows your ability to love
- Shows your soul's need to rest and rejuvenate
- Shows you an opportunity for deeper acceptance of impermanence of each moment
- Shows you an opportunity to ask for help or lean on others

Shadows of grief:

- Shows you your attachment to experiences
- Can lead to escapism if not properly addressed
- Can trigger other negative emotions
- Can lead to victim mentality

Grief is another universal emotion. Grief asks us, "What has left our current reality that we have become accustomed to?" Loss of "something" in this reality could mean a number of things: the passing of a loved one, loss of a romantic relationship, loss of a friendship, loss of a job, loss of a car from an accident, loss of a pet, etc. Notice that grief can show us where we are letting go of a social role we played in respect to the loss. When you break up with someone, you are no longer identifying as their romantic partner. Then your identity as a boyfriend or a girlfriend is lost. And notice that this is what you're truly grieving. The love or the connection existed aren't what's being lost. Grief is the evidence of connection and love that exist, just in a changed form. Grief just gently asks us to surrender to the changes in life and detach each moment. Grief asks us to focus on healing our hearts. So, when grief arises, be gentle with yourself. Set an intention to feel it rather than avoiding it or numbing it. Imagine that grief is like a river that you notice flowing through in front of you. Rather than pretending that it is not there, go into the river. Let the flowing river of emotions wash and heal you. Be with grief, and notice that it is showing you the ability for you to love. One way to allow grief to wash over you is to journal about what comes up for you feeling this grief and what you learned from the experience of being with the thing or the person that you are grieving. Allow this gratitude to heal you and nurture you.

Exercise for When You Feel Grief

Here is an exercise to help you cope with grief.

1. Come to a comfortable sitting position.
2. Bring your hands to your heart center, palms together in a praying position and gently close your eyes.
3. Ask yourself, "What am I grieving?"
4. Hold the image of the person, thing, idea, business, pets, etc. in your mind with love. If it is a person, invite the healthiest, brightest moment or image you have of them in your mind's eye, and as the person smiles, imagine bright divine light shining on them to bless their being. (Although this prayer works for anything you are grieving, specifically for the loss of a person, it will help calm your mind and heart. If it is a thing, momentarily

remember a bright moment that you associate with that thing or event.)

5. Now imagine you are filling your entire being with radiating light.
6. Connect to your highest self, your divine source, by stating, "I gently request healing light and compassion for my grieving heart as I surrender and let go of what it was. Thank you for having gifted me the beautiful experience with ______. "

Now say the following prayer if grieving a person:

Thank you, Infinitely Loving Universe for allowing me to have co-created my life with ______.

I am infinitely grateful that I have the memories, love, and connection I shared with _____ at any time, for love is not bound by time or space. I surrender to you, Infinitely Loving Universe, as I wholeheartedly trust that you take care of all souls in all states of the journey. You take over. You take over. You take over. I surrender to you. Thank you.

Shame

Positive intent of shame:

- Gives motivation to take responsibility and change behavior to restore integrity and power
- Activator to heal relationships
- Shows you where you can close a gap for who you're being and who you say you're being in the world

Shadows of shame:

- Shows up as inability to separate our worth from our behaviors to our soul (i.e. our behavior might have not been ideal, but that doesn't change the worth of our soul)
- Lowest vibrational frequency and doesn't contribute to abundant, creative energy on its own, until action is taken to move out of shame (such as apologizing and ownership where integrity was lacking)
- Can drain energy

Shame validates that you are an emotionally healthy human with the ability to access a wide range of emotions. Shame feels like embarrassment, a need to hide, a desire to "cover up." Shame shows up when you feel you have exposed for the first time who you really are. It is uncomfortable because it requires you to sit with who you really are in contrast to who others think you should be. It stems from the idea that we won't be accepted exactly as who we are. According to Brené Brown (brenebrown.com) , a researcher and speaker on the emotion of shame, at the core of shame, the foundational belief is that "we are not good enough."

What is shame's purpose? Its positive intent is recognition that your soul is asking you to forgive and love yourself unconditionally. It is kindly asking you to let go of the judgments you hold toward yourself. It is also asking you to free yourself from others' judgments. It is asking you to practice compassion for yourself. It gently reminds you that the only one who gets to judge you is Infinite Intelligence, the Universe, a higher being.

The next time shame shows up, I invite you to allow the love, compassion, and forgiveness through you. Thank the shame as it passes through your body and mind. Shame can show up as the immediate side effect of being vulnerable. Have you ever shared something that you don't typically share with somebody, and the immediate thoughts after was, "are they going to judge me? Will they accept me? Will they think I am weird?" This is because oftentimes, when we open up and show parts of ourselves that we have been hiding, we feel a pang of shame after. Instead, try on being proud of yourself for being courageous enough to be open and acknowledge your authentic self. Notice the discomfort that shows up after being open and remind yourself that you are enough. Congratulate yourself for taking the first step in becoming aware of who you really are at your core and owning who you truly are. So when you notice shame, notice that it is not there to stay forever. Acknowledge it, and remind yourself, "I am loved. I am perfect in my imperfections. I love all of me."

Exercise for When You Feel Shame

This is a simple body-mind-breath exercise that opens your heart to the possibilities, expanding your authentic self loudly to express your full self and owning your power. It also allows your body to move energy around intuitively as it is activated by your breath to heal and nurture you.

- Take a seat or stand up for this breathing exercise. Set your intention on sending intense infinite love to your body. Close your eyes.
- Inhale deeply through your nose and fill up your lungs fully with gratitude, opening and stretching your arms and fingers wide out around you, taking up as much space as you possibly can.
- Audibly exhale through your mouth, letting all your air out, and lowering your arms gently next to your torso or forming prayer hands in front of you.
- Inhale again through your nose with your arms and palms spread wide, fully expressing and expanding yourself
- Exhale loudly, letting any movement or sound release.
- Add any other movements that feel good as you victoriously inhale through your nose again.
- Exhale expressively as you shake out your body to release any tension, imagining your being melting into the Earth's nurturing.
- Let your body, your voice, your movements express themselves in all the ways that feel most authentic, loud, and creative.
- Take another deep inhale through your nose.
- Every time you inhale, imagine powerful energy in the form of golden light being invited deeply into your body. It is entering and empowering all parts of your body—your heart, lungs, brain, arms and legs, and stomach

- Exhale all the air as you imagine light shooting out of your fingers and body to create a bright aura around you.
- Continue this exercise for five to ten minutes.

Anxiety

Positive intent of anxiety:

- Shows you that you have a creative mind and that your mind is imagining an outcome that hasn't happened
- Shows you you care about something a lot
- Calls for you to come back to the present moment
- Shows you where you can surrender more

Shadows of anxiety:

- Anxiety is draining energy that takes you away from being powerful in the present moment
- Anxiety is fear-based energy
- Anxiety stunts your creativity

Anxiety happens when you're not being present in the moment. When you feel anxiety, you may be thinking about the past or future. Anxiety is focusing on things that cannot be changed or you have no control over. Anxiety may also result from too much pent-up energy or emotion of any sort that you haven't fully expressed. For instance, if you feel ecstatic joy, but you don't feel safe expressing it, it may lead to anxiety. Anxiety results from prolonged stress and may make you enter fight or flight mode.

Anxiety's positive intent is to remind you that your body wants you to come back home, to feel nurtured and comforted, and to be loved. It invites you to come back to your body in this present moment. When you are stuck in the past, anxiety results because you cannot control or change anything. If you have anxiety about the future, it is not helpful because you cannot control what hasn't happened yet. The present moment is the only place you can truly access peace and ease because it is a place of possibility and gratitude; anything is possible in the current moment, and you can always find gratitude in this present moment in your body because it means you are alive. You can honor anxiety's purpose by remembering it allowed you to tap into your awareness of not feeling present, secure, and comfortable.

Exercise for When You Feel Anxiety

This exercise helps with anxiety through a self-sufficient somatosensory technique that promotes oxytocin in your body. Oxytocin is the hormone that gets released through touch and connection. You can access the release of oxytocin in your own body by nurturing yourself. This meditation allows you to be in a position of nurturing yourself while reminding yourself that you are safe in your own body and can tap into the present moment at any time. It helps if you have peaceful piano music you can play in the background or on your headphones.

- Get into a comfortable sitting position. You may lean against a wall or sit up straight. You can even sit comfortably on a couch or lie on your back.

- Inhale deeply through your nose and exhale completely through your mouth very slowly.
- Place both of your hands on your heart.
- Imagine that you are blessing your heart and your entire body, and that white infinitely loving light surrounds you.
- Continue slowly breathing through your nose and out through your mouth for the rest of the exercise. Close your eyes for added relaxation. Imagine that every time you breathe in, the healing white light surrounding you gets into your body and relaxes you. Every time you exhale, imagine that you are letting all the stagnant energy out of your body.
- Continue this exercise until you feel peace and calmness in your body. For best results, do it for at least fifteen minutes each session.

Feel free to go to www.creatingyourownhappiness.com to get additional meditation resources.

The Rest: Creative and Abundant Emotions

The absence of these aforementioned emotions such as fear, anxiety, anger, shame and guilt, are creative, love, abundance and expansion oriented emotions such as **optimism, happiness, joy, peace and unconditional love.**

Positive intent of creative emotions

- Love energy
- Source energy

- Life giving
- Creates connection
- Calls for the most natural state of our being, a state of creativity
- Energy giving and pulls towards a vision
- Creates abundance
- Creates win-win
- Shows the magic of the present moment
- Creates unity, harmony and synergy

Shadows of creative emotions

- Desire to want to hold onto an emotion, rather than continue to detach and surrender to the impermanence of each emotion (i.e. I am joyful now, and I want to be joyful forever)
- Important to consciously and compassionately become empathetic to those stuck in the fear-based emotions

While most would think, what shadows can exist for "creative and abundant" emotions, I have listed a few here. The lesson here is that no matter what emotion, there is a positive intent as well as a shadow to every emotion. And light and shadow to everything in the Universe. That is the divine dichotomy of this Universe that exists in everything.

The shadows of these emotions are that you get to remind yourself that, like any other emotions, these emotions will flow, and will not be permanent, just like the fear-based emotions as listed above this section. Not being mindful about this can create an unhealthy attachment to wanting these emotions to last forever. An unwillingness to accept their impermanence can cause people to turn to addictions or unhealthy behaviors to suppress darker emotions and stay in these creative emotions longer. The benefits of staying in these emotions is you get to access the creator in you, you get to create your life, and you get to enjoy the process of moving toward and accomplishing your goals.

The most important thing to realize here is that no emotions are good or bad, right or wrong. All emotions happen exactly as they should. Through practice observing your mind and energy, however, you can start to find unshakable joy and peace in your heart, regardless of what's happening in the external world. And by understanding the positive intent and the shadow of each emotion, we get an opportunity to get away from judging if an emotion is "positive" or "negative," and rather, we get to take in the lesson from each emotion and express it in a conscious way that expands us, rather than causes destruction or conflicts in our lives. And this way, we get to express, and not suppress, our emotions, and at the same time, know that we don't have to be attached to them in any way. We get to let them flow through us, like any other experiences that life offers us. And when we can flow with these emotions, rather than get stuck in life because of them, we get to live a life accessing more freedom and fulfillment.

Journal Exercise

What are you learning about your emotions from this chapter? How will you apply your understanding of emotions in your own life?

____

____

What emotions are present with you today, in this moment? How can you let this emotion guide you towards your best self, based on what you're learning about them from above?

CHAPTER 24

EXPRESSING YOUR INTENTIONS

Why do I do what I do?
Why do I do what I do?
Why do I do what I do?
— y.c.

I don't exactly know when it was or where I was, but I remember I asked myself this question, "Why do I do what I do?" This was one simple, yet powerful question. I believe this is when I started to notice that there may be a separation between what my body is conditioned to do and that I have a choice.

Do you know *why* you do all the things you do in life? Do you know why you are going to work? Do you know why you buy the things that you do? What about the automatic behaviors or habits like why you brush your teeth the way that you do? Why do you eat the same kind of food every morning without thinking about it? Why do you wear the clothes you do?

Know & Express Your Intentions

My clients often tell me, by working with me, they learn what it truly means to live an "intentional life." An intention is your "*true* why" and the energy behind why you do what you do. It is the *real* reason you took that action or said something. When your intention comes from your soul, it adds to the natural expansion and abundance flow of the Universe. According to Dr. Wayne Dyer, an intention is "a force in the universe that allows the act of creation to take place." When you speak with an intention that aligns with who you really are, you are speaking and letting your soul be expressed in those actions or your words. It is important though to set your intention then detach from the outcome of that intention. For example, my intention for writing this book for you, is that when you read it, you are deeply inspired to transform yourself towards your best version of yourself and to find joy along that journey. If my intention gets delivered and communicated to you in the way I intended as you read this, then I know my soul's message reached your soul. But there is a chance that you interpret the message of this book in a different way, and it doesn't end up inspiring you. I get to detach from that outcome and focus on my intention of inspiration and transformation because this intention is all I have control over. In this, I eliminate room for disappointment or desire to control what I cannot control. I get to focus on who I am *being* and the energy I am putting out to the Universe regardless of the outcome. When we take a moment to set an intention for each moment, over time, we are putting together the building blocks of living a truly intentional life, one that is purposeful, fulfilling and expansive.

When people act without intentions the world becomes disconnected, stagnant and chaotic. People do things out of habit, or on auto-pilot, or they live in a reactionary mode without thinking about why they do what they do. When there are no intentions set for why people do what they do, it diminishes the opportunity to take mindful actions and live consciously. When I asked one of my clients on our first call as we discussed his partying habits that he wanted to change, I asked him this question: "Why do you drink or party?" And he thought about it for a while, and he said "you know, I've never thought about that. I don't even know why. I guess I have just been partying just because that's what everyone does on the weekends in my friends' group. But I haven't really thought about why." When he dug deeper, he said "I think I drink because I am bored and because I am stressed. And sometimes I drink because I want to have more fun or feel confident. Wow, saying that out loud, I am realizing that these aren't good reasons to drink or party." Once he got clear that he had been partying all these years without even knowing why, or his intentions behind it, he realized that he wanted to ditch his mindless partying habit and replace it with better habits. But prior to being intentional about his partying habits or eliminating them, he felt stuck and stagnant. This is because over time, when we continually engage in non-intentional, mindless activities, we start to lose our connection to our souls. Our souls start to get buried under layers and layers of careless and meaningless activities when done without intentions. The soul suffers as life feels meaningless. That is when people start to feel disconnected and lonely. They feel depressed. They forget why they do what they are doing. They forget why they are living. And instead of your soul, your ego takes the lead of your life. Intentional living is what helps the soul breathe. Intentions allow our souls to be expressed fully into this reality. Intentions give our souls a voice in what we put out to the world energetically. Choosing an intention allows us to be a non-robot. Choosing an intention allows us to create and choose new possibilities.

Choosing an intention is a key ingredient in living a fulfilling, happy life.

Exercise: What is your intention? Pick one word of intention for: today, the week, the month and the year

*For today:*____

For the week: ____________________________________

For the month: __________________________________

For the year: _____________________________________

Chapter 25

Leading with Your Soul

Your soul, always,
already knows
what's the best thing
to do in every situation.
It just silently sits and watches
how much your ego
can tempt you
to do other things.
— y.c.

Your Ego Offers You Nothing Towards What You Truly Want

Can you surrender and listen to your soul in silence, rather than the loudness of your ego? Can you see that your ego was created by your mind, but your soul was created by something bigger and greater? Do you know that your soul rejoices in your joy, and your ego dissolves in your joy?

3 Signs Your Ego is Trying to Take Over

Your ego is a protective mechanism that was created to protect your identity and different ideas about who you are. Ego isn't necessarily a bad thing; it's just that when people let their ego take over their lives, diminishing the light of their souls, it can start to cause their lives to not "work" as well and they feel less fulfilled. Here, I'd like to share with you

3 signs that you can become aware of when your ego starts to take over your life, so that you can actively come back to your heart and your soul again if you start to notice these things happening.

1. Comparison

When you find yourself comparing yourself to others and starting to come from a place of who's better or worse, too much or not enough, and so on, notice it. Become aware of the fact that this is your ego at work and trying to take over your life. When you find yourself starting to compare, remember to come back to your heart, and remember to come back to love. There is truly no hierarchy when it comes to any souls; we are all made equal, and we are all perfect, whole, and complete in different ways.

2. Conflicts

Egos collide and end up in conflicts; souls unite and celebrate in love. When ego is trying to take over your life, you will start to see unnecessary clashing happening with other people. Ego wants to know that one of you is wrong, and the other one is right. This is also coming from a place of judgement. Notice this and remember that we all get to have a life of harmony and love, if we choose to.

3. Fear

Fear for the most part, is an imaginary concept. Fear in our bodies truly exists to help us out of physically dangerous situations, so that we can survive in our physical bodies as mentioned in an earlier chapter. However, as we started to form our egos, fear arises because we want to protect our identities from social situations, whether it is fear of rejection or fear of being excluded from a tribe. When fear starts to arise, and we are not in physical danger, I invite you to become aware that fear is starting to arise as a way of ego to take over your life. When this starts to happen, we start to operate from a fight, flight or freeze mode - and when it is coming from a social situation, it is not helpful as far as living a powerfully, fearless life, leading with our hearts. So next time you start to notice any of this happening, remember what we are truly made of love (not our egos!).

Showing Up with Love When It's Most Difficult

So, when you feel disconnected from your soul, it may be because your ego is getting in the way. In these moments, try asking this question: "What is my ego trying to protect, that it doesn't need to, and can just love instead?" And ask yourself, "If I showed up with love right now, instead of fear, what new possibilities could I create towards my best self?"

Showing up with love, when fear wants to rule our lives, creates defining moments in relationships and situations. Those moments get alchemized from a destructive state, to an abundant state. It calls for the energy of courage to transmute fear into love. This is the very moment when your ego dies, and your soul rises. When you feel like running away from a difficult conversation, can you turn around and show up and stay there? When you feel like shutting down, can you open your heart and lean in? When you feel like your ego is trying to say things you don't mean, can you consciously set ego aside, say exactly what you mean, and just love harder? Leading life from a place of love frees you from your fears, or your ego, trying to dominate your life, and leads to an expansive, abundant life, leading to more happiness.

Journaling Exercise

1. Think about a time recently that you experienced your ego, or your fear-based energy, that led your experience. Journal below.

____

____

____

2. If you were to approach this same situation with love, instead of leading with your ego, what would that have looked like?

____

____

____

CHAPTER 26

EXPRESSING GRATITUDE

if you are reading this,
you have eyes that can see,
you have a brain that can
comprehend words,
you have a heart that beats,
you have a soul that feels,
you have a life to be lived,
if you are reading this,
we already have so much
in common and so much
to celebrate today.

— y.c.

How many times a day do you think about what you're grateful for? Did you know that research is finding more and more evidence that when expressing or receiving gratitude, our brains release more of the happy neurotransmitters, such as dopamine and serotonin? In 2018, Joel Wong & a group of researchers assigned subjects into 3 groups. One group was receiving psychotherapy only. Another group was receiving psychotherapy and was asked to journal about their stressful experiences from the day to express whatever came to their mind, and the last group was receiving psychotherapy and asked to do a gratitude journal highlighting what they are thankful for. They found that the "gratitude" group reported feeling more positive feelings, such as empathy and kindness, leaving them significantly happier than the other two groups. Other research has found that this is due to the fact that gratitude changed the brain so that more dopamine was released from the brain stem, leaving people happier. So, beautiful soul, can we pause for a bit? Take a deep breath in, and exhale, right now as you read this, and ask this simple question that changes the chemical within your brain to be happier: "What are you thankful for today?"

Gratitude is My Favorite Attitude

Back in 2012 on Christmas Day, my friends and I did something different from what we usually do (which is eating a lot and going into a food coma at home). We went to help feed the homeless at a park in Anaheim. It was a surprisingly beautiful, sunny day, easily reaching 75 degrees in December. I used to live in Colorado in my teen years where I had to get used to the snow, wind, and bitter coldness in the winter times, so this really was an absolutely unbelievable winter morning and the only thing against my face was the welcoming sunshine's warmth.

More than thirty volunteers came to serve brunch, and instantly, we all bonded over being at a park together on Christmas morning. A small neighborhood church had already brought food for us to serve. We set up a few long tables to resemble a buffet. Everyone was given different bowls of food—stuffing, turkey, casserole, etc. I was given a big bowl of rice to serve.

The homeless people, whom I believe resided at the park, started walking down the buffet line to get a little scoop of everything. They were all unique in their own ways. There was an older gentleman with hair that hadn't been washed in months, and ladies in broken walkers. Some of them were just hilarious! One guy told me he didn't want any more stuffing because he was on a low-carb diet, then walked away chuckling at his own joke. (I didn't know if I should laugh or not.) Another asked me if I was hiding any teriyaki chicken under my coat (I wasn't wearing a coat) to go with the rice.

One toothless lady exclaimed, "This place is a paradise! Look at the weather and look at this blessed day!" as she eagerly took her plate of food from us and sat down on the green grass next to our serving tables to eat her meal. She meant it; her big smile revealed her true thankfulness for being alive, being fed, and just simply being around people on Christmas Day at her park. She looked happier in that moment than most people I know with homes. In her gratitude, she was happy, beautiful and abundant.

I share this story is a reminder that we can always find a way to find gratitude, regardless of our situation. Although those people that day didn't have that much, in gratitude, they were creating their own happiness. The irony is that, at times, the more we have, the easier it is to forget to be grateful for them all. Yet gratitude is the portal to instant joy, at any time.

Happiness is subjective and relative, and things that can make us happy are all around us. When we slow down and come back to gratitude, anger, fear, resentment all can subside immediately. When in doubt, get in the habit of asking, what am I grateful for right now, and notice your energy shift immediately into something light and expansive. Stay there. This is your nature. This is who you really are.

Healing Through Gratitude

"What part of your body are you really insecure about?" A guy I met once asked me this. While I thought it a weird question, with an open mind and trying not to judge the question, I checked in with my body to see what my truth was to this question. I closed my eyes. Hmm, let's do a scan. Was it…

My hair…?

I remember when my dad was going through intensive chemo…and started losing his hair. (He didn't have much to lose to begin with. He would always joke about that.) I am so grateful my hair is long and grows steadily, as if it is the evidence of my health.

My eyes…?

Ha! When I first moved to the U.S. at age eleven, I was insecure because my eyes looked different from everyone else's. I thought Western eyes were so beautiful, but mine were not. As a teenager, people would make comments about "chinky eyes" that used to make me feel small. Over the years, however, I have really come to love my almond-shaped eyes and learned to accept myself as I am. I also used to have to wear contacts and glasses, but now that I got LASIK, I am so thankful for my perfect vision.

My lips, my mouth…?

When I got my tonsils out, everything I ate felt like I was eating razors. Today, I can taste the flavors of all foods, and I am so grateful that I can eat, chew, swallow, and feel good.

My boobs…?

When I was thirteen, I was supposed to "grow" my boobs. As a teenager, I really wanted bigger boobs. One day, after a yoga class in my late twenties, I just decided my boobs were perfect for me. I giggled as I imagined how difficult headstands would be if my boobs were super big and came up to my neck when I was upside down. Hahaha! That visual made me laugh out loud. I'd probably fall over because I wouldn't know how to balance them! I love my boobs so much today. I am thankful they are healthy.

My stomach…?

My dad's stomach would get filled with fluid during the last few months of his cancer battle. We would have to transport him to the ER every two days just to release the fluid by sticking a needle into his stomach to extract it. It looked so painful. I promised myself I would never take my stomach and health for granted. I am so grateful for my stomach and all it does for me.

My legs…?

When I was seven, I broke my left leg. I felt miserable being immobile and having to wear a cast. I decided I would never take my legs or ability to walk for granted! And I haven't forgotten it.

My weight…?

I get a little emotional when I remember being eighteen and thinking I was never skinny enough, pretty enough, or enough in general. I used to punish and torture my body and self this way.

I got a little teary-eyed thinking about how much I've grown, how much I've healed, and how much I learned to love myself. I wanted to hug myself! Now, as I sat in front of this person, answering his odd question, I was thankful to be reminded that I feel grateful and beautiful.

"I think I am really just grateful for my body," I told him, and I meant it wholeheartedly.

My response made him sort of panic, and he replied, "You can't be telling the truth. You've gotta have a place on your body you pick apart. Everyone has some sort of insecurity about their body."

I smiled. He didn't know the power of gratitude yet.

*****

Our bodies are vehicles for our souls. They are where our souls live for a handful of decades. The body wasn't created to be judged or compared. It certainly was not created for us to hate. It was not created for us to abuse and neglect. It is simply a place where your soul gets to enjoy this precious journey of life. When insecurities arise, try on surrendering to gratitude, and what your body and health actually do for you. Can you be deeply grateful for your body's health, for its abilities, for all it does for you, for all it allows your soul to experience during your life?

Gratitude Exercise

What can you be grateful for right now? Even if you're having the worst day, I can help you find things to be grateful for. Here are some examples:

1. I am thankful for the abundance of this Universe. There is always water, air, wind, ocean, and they are all free.

2. I am thankful for my ability to read this.
3. I am thankful for language that allows humans to connect, communicate, and co-create together.
4. I am thankful for love from my family and the Universe.
5. I am thankful for wealth that manifests in my life.
6. I am thankful for my health and my breaths.
7. I am thankful for all of my internal organs that support me every day the best they can.
8. I am thankful for my creativity.
9. I am thankful for my ability to serve others.
10. I am thankful for my life!

I invite you to create your own gratitude list. If possible, create one every day to invite more beautiful things into your life.

Universe is truly conspiring for your happiness and the best version of you, if you look for the signs and ways. What you choose to focus on and speak about have the power to either add to or subtract from your happiness. When you genuinely appreciate something, the Universe gives you more of whatever you are appreciating. People do the same. When you show appreciation for something they did for you, they are more willing to help you again. However, if you complain after they tried to help, they probably won't want to ever help you again. Therefore, gratitude attracts more of what you want. Complaining attracts more of what you don't want. Neither are good or bad; you simply have the power to choose your quality of life with each word you speak.

Exercise

1. What are you grateful for today that you might easily take for granted? List ten things you are grateful for below.

1. ______________________________

2. ______________________________

3. ______________________________

4. ______________________________

5. ______________________________

6. ______________________________

7. ______________________________

8. ______________________________

9. ______________________________

10. ______________________________

2. What are three things you are grateful for in the last 365 days?

____

____

____

3. Who are three people you are grateful for? Think of three people that you haven't spoken to in the last 3 months, and list them here.

____

____

____

Bonus Exercise: Reach out to these three people via text, call or email today, and share your gratitude with them directly.

4. What ability or gift of yours are you most grateful for?

____

____

____

CHAPTER 27

DECLARING YOUR DESIRES AND VISIONS

They can...
Turn strangers into friends
comfort a heart in pain
show love
start a war
save a life
ignite lust
heal the wounded
forgive others.
words,
they can.
— y.c.

Declare Your Vision

Look around you. Everything around you was once just a thought in someone's head. The chair you are sitting on as you read this, was a thought in someone's head. Then they either told a team of designers or created a blueprint to communicate his vision. They created that thought first, then shared that vision with others, so that the right people and resources can come together to support that vision to come to reality.

Often, we let our ideas stay where they popped up: in our heads and in our internal world. And we forget to participate in the most important step in the process of creating our reality—a step that allows other people to share your internal world. That step is: expressing and declaring your vision out loud to other people.

Two things happen when we declare our visions. One is that our words themselves are powerful spells. You are essentially creating a verbal agreement with the Universe and with yourself that vision is going to happen. This holds you accountable subconsciously as we, for the most part, have the natural tendency to be in integrity with our words. Second is that now other people are giving your vision more energy as you share with them, and now, they are also thinking about it. "Giving energy" to your vision could also look like them fueling the literal energy for this vision to manifest, by providing you with funds, connections, resources, to actually make your vision happen in real life, as fast as possible.

Below, I share a personal story that shows the power of declaring and sharing my visions with other people. Magic can happen at a quantum speed, when you trust the Universe that it will support your visions and dreams to come true.

Saying Yes to My Vision to Become a Speaker

A few years ago, I was at a transformational seminar where we were called to declare a vision we had for ourselves that we have never shared publicly before. Up until then, I had never admitted to anyone that I wanted to be a speaker. I had all these self- deprecating thoughts about what it meant for me to admit that up until then.

So in front of 120 people at the seminar, I declared my vision. I declared it out loud, despite my fears of being judged and looking stupid. I declared, "I want to be a speaker because I am ready to speak out loud about my mission to bring more love and ease into this world and contribute to eliminating dis-ease." Have you ever had dreams that seemed so big and out there for you, that it was hard for you to share initially? I felt so nervous sharing this!

The events that followed were magical and synchronistic. Within one week, I was invited to a speakers' birthday party by my friend Christina. When she told me and invited me to the party, my body felt at "ease" and "joyful" (some of my core values as listed earlier), so without much analyzing or without too much information about the speaker, I said yes. It was a full body yes. This, on a logical level, was bizarre because the party was 2.5 hours away from where I was, yet thinking about going there energized me. To my surprise, it turned out to be a private birthday party for the legendary motivational speaker, Les Brown. And there, I met many successful speakers and authors, who quickly became my friends. Then from a friend I met there, I manifested the opportunity to attend *The Secret Knock,* an incredible event full of speakers and powerful entrepreneurs —both among the speakers and in the audience! Then one connection led to another, and within two weeks, I manifested a meeting with Erik Swanson, the Founder of the Habitude Warrior Conference. In our first meeting, the first question he asked me was, "What is your vision?"

Prior to that seminar I attended, I never would have had the courage to say I wanted to be a speaker. Now, I found myself saying just that to Erik accessing courage. "My dream is to be a speaker. I am ready to be a speaker and spread my message of love, ease, compassion, and joy from the stage anywhere. I want to help millions of people."

Erik looked at me as I spoke with so much certainty and said, "There is a two-year waiting list to be on my stage. But something tells me that I want to support your dreams. Do you want to be one of my MC's and on my Women Empowerment Panel? If you say yes now, I will buy your ticket and room for you to come right now."

I looked at my calendar. The event was the weekend I was supposed to have a girls' night out with some of my best friends in Scottsdale. Even though I had just declared this so powerfully, so much that I manifested the very thing I wanted, I found myself hesitating.

"But I might…have to go to this thing in Scottsdale…."

"Let me tell you something. And this is something I learned over the years. If this is something you really want to do, and will take you towards your vision, then say yes. That's all you have to know."

I quickly realized the Universe was trying to give me exactly what I had asked for, and in the moment of receiving, I had almost accidentally rejected it. I quickly realized this decision aligned with my vision and my core values of following my joy and my courage. I smiled, "Yes! Let's do this!"

I was shaking with excitement, and a little bit of fear. Could I really be good on stage? Could I do this when I'd never done it before? I could and I did! Not only did it go amazingly, but I have had the honor of being on Erik's stage ever since, and have shared the stage with legends like Brian Tracy (International Best Selling Author, author of over 70 books, and Global Motivational Speaker) , Sharon Lechter (Co-Author of Rich Dad, Poor Dad, Official Annotator for *Outwitting the Devil,* President's Council for Financial Literacy for Bush & Obama Administration), Frank Shankwitz (Co-Founder of *Make-A-Wish Foundation)*, Greg Reid (*Founder of Secret Knock)* and many more because of that one yes. And I ended up making it work to create a possibility of attending both this event as well as the later part of the girls' weekend.

In that moment, I learned something important forever: the power of sharing my vision and declaring it to the Universe. When it feels a little scary and massively exciting all at the same time to share your deepest desires and vision, that's when you know you are declaring something that is valuable to you. And when you do, the Universe conspires for your vision and for your ultimate happiness.

Exercise

1. Declare here your vision or a new possibility below that you've never shared with anyone before.

____

____

____

____

____

2. Why have you never shared this vision or idea with anyone before?

3. Pick 3 people to share this vision with today. Who did you share it with? How did it feel to share? Journal below.

Part V

CONNECTION

CHAPTER 28

CONNECTING TO SELF

"how do I bring
more Happiness to you,
Universe?"
Universe gave me a mirror.
"there's your assignment.
heal. love. forgive. forever.
And that's your only assignment."
— y.c.

Why is it important to connect to self? What does that mean? We can't give what we don't have. If we cannot source the feeling of connection back to self, we cannot offer the feeling of connection to others. We cannot readily receive what we're not used to having, so lack of connection to self can also lead to lack of creating connection with others as well. First, let's look at the risk of not making time to connect with oneself.

Why Some Charismatic, Successful People Suffer From Loneliness and Emptiness: Connecting Back to Your Soul

Robin Williams, Marilyn Monroe, and Kate Spade were well-liked, charismatic, and successful, so what happened to them? What led each of them to blow out their own radiant light? What led them to get so lost in darkness that they took their own lives? Consider for a second that charisma, creative, happy or any other "personality" aspect of a person is just a decoration, makeup, or mask to your soul, unless you're truly being it. The key here is lack of deep connection to self. When you're not truly *being* the joy, the freedom, the charisma, but you *act* like it, the disconnection is hard for your soul.

Charismatic personality, sexy personality, creative personality, funny personality—whatever these people identified themselves with is what got them to being successful, famous, well-liked, influential, wealthy, and so on. So of course, the ego doesn't want to let go of these personalities because it works to get what the ego wants, neglecting their soul. But then, they unintentionally trap their souls under their personalities by mistake. When their soul is trapped deep down, people lose their ability to "come home" to themselves. So one day, their soul suffocates to the point of no return.

Your ego creates your personality to dictate how others perceive you so you can look good, be understood, and be accepted by other egos. The doings of ego isn't wrong, good, bad, or right. But we cannot forget that putting on a personality is an act driven by ego, to get you what's important to your ego in this physical world: success, fame, popularity, influence, material wealth. But your soul doesn't care about any of that. Your soul just wants you to grow, be joyful, and to love. Your soul loves it when you self-express fully and be all of you brightly: your individuality, and in your sacred uniqueness. Just like your clothes and makeup, your personality is just another decoration that hides and decorates who you really are on a soul level.

While we regularly take off our clothes or makeup to refresh, how often do we take off our personalities, so our soul can have a moment to breathe and cleanse itself? The soul breathes and rejuvenates, and connects to the rest of the Universe through: *art, love, meditation, music, dancing, singing, laughter, deep connection and play.*

Soul celebrates in any way that gives it the opportunity to create, express itself, and be free. Embody your joy and creative flow, if you wish to connect to your soul.

When you don't connect to your soul and let your soul express itself, but let it be trapped under your rigid masks of your "personality" to please the world, you don't let your soul breathe, it suffocates; the soul gets so sad and lonely that it decays, in this unbreathable container, of your personality. Let your soul breathe. And don't let your soul suffer. Let yourself connect to your soul. Just as our lungs need oxygen, just as our bodies need showers, just as our skin needs to breathe, our soul needs to know that you are there searching for it and that you are doing the work to get to know it. And when you want to connect back to your soul remember this. Your soul is expressed through your joy. Your soul is expressed through your creativity.

Self-Love: Connecting to My Body, My Home for my Soul

When I say "home," what comes to your mind? Your parents' home that you grew up in? The city you were born in? Your family? Your hometown where you grew up? Where do you live now? Your significant other? Your kids? Your family? What is "home" for you?

For me, it is not as simple as the place I was born or grew up in. For years, I didn't know where I could say, "Yes, I am unconditionally loved, completely accepted and safe." I've lived in 2 countries, have lived in 3 different states in the U.S., and many different cities. And even within each city, I have moved *many* times. I have mastered the art of entering then, learning and observing the environment, adapting to, experiencing, and expanding in the new environment, then getting up and starting over: moving again, learning again, becoming aware again, adapting again, and all over again.

I got used to being good at adapting and quickly assimilating to a new culture to "fit in." *I had mastered the art of being a social chameleon.* In high school, I came across a quote that gave me immense comfort in being a social chameleon: "The only constant is change." I loved that. But while it gave me temporary comfort, it also confused me because since I was constantly changing and adapting, I had a hard time understanding where my authentic self actually dwelled and where my true home was for my soul. It was hard for me to feel truly grounded for a while. (Back then, I wasn't clear of my core values or my vision.) I was so good at adapting and changing, but who was I really? So where is my home for me?

Meanwhile, a few years ago, I started to search for home by starting a relationship and connection to the Universe. I began to notice more and more the beauty and unconditional love that surrounds me all the time, which started to help me feel grounded, nurtured, and safe. I started to slowly find the constant change of the Universe to be comforting. But this feeling of home was sometimes fleeting. Sometimes

I questioned my faith due to different hardships, and sometimes, I simply didn't feel present enough to find this security through my trust in the Universe.

Then I had an epiphany one day a few years back. I found something that was truly and completely a place of safety, something that serves as a constant, and a place of complete acceptance that I had overlooked all these years. And it was not a place. It wasn't a house. It wasn't even family or other people. It wasn't as vague as "the Universe." It was much easier than that. I found it stretching on my yoga mat one day. I love yoga. Yoga is something that's been a huge part of my life. It is something I realize I have started to find comfort and security in, because no matter what was going on in my life, it made me feel good when I surrendered to yoga.

And I realized it wasn't even "yoga" that was my home. Yoga was just the door for me to enter my home. My home was and is...what was on the yoga mat, and with me all along: my own physical body and my authentic being. Today I know where my home is. It was when I was 100% accepting of my authentic self and 100% in love with my body, that is simply a vehicle for my soul's mission, that's when I started to feel home, anywhere. And my authentic being is that part that doesn't have to be chameleonic because it is already perfect. My authentic being is the part that seems quirky because I am not changing parts of me to fit into social norms. My authentic being is the part I can just come home to because it is the most natural and comfortable place on earth.

I will continue to change—no doubt—but no longer at the expense of losing my home. My driving force is "growth" after all. But my home will stay the same. It consists of my unwavering values, my purpose in deeply helping people, and my love for others. My home secures my stable foundation no matter what.

I am coming home to my body today.

I am coming home to my breath.

I am coming home to my beating heart.

I am coming home to my body…which is my soul's home.

And all I have to do to come home is to place my hand on my heart and breathe. I rest easy in this nest. I am happy to be home today.

Listening and Connecting to Self through Meditation

Sit. Cross your legs. Close your eyes. Extend your spine. Come to your sitting meditation. In silence, we get to turn off the noise of everything that is not actually us. Mindfulness is the glue to bring your body and your soul to a place of union. I can actively invite love, connection and the surrender to the present moment back into my body through meditation.

Today, I invite you to put your hand on your heart, or your tummy, or wherever your hand intuitively leads you to, and breathe. Imagine that every breath you take, you are sending gratitude toward each area of your body, both internal and external.

Thank your lungs, your heart, your stomach, and all your organs that seem to function amazingly every second without having to conduct them all separately. Thank your brain. Thank your facial muscles, which allows you to smile, cry, laugh, and fully express all of my emotions.

Maybe you pick one body part a day, and every time you have a free moment, you fill your mind with gratitude for that part of your body. Then, the next day, you pick another body part and intently send love to it. Within 365 days, I would imagine more parts of your body would receive active love from you than not. Imagine how much your body would love you back for that.

Today, connect to yourself. Come home to yourself.

"Mindfulness helps you go home to the present.
And every time you go there and recognize
a condition of happiness that you have,
happiness comes."
— Thich Nhat Hanh

Exercise: Connecting to Self Meditation

Thank you, Universe, for this moment of healing. Thank you, Universe, for creating this amazing body that allows me to manifest all I desire into the physical world. Thank you, Universe, for this amazing ease and radiating light I feel all over my body. Thank you, Universe, for allowing me to come back home to my soul.

(Find more guided meditations on creatingyourownhappiness.com)

Journal about a time that you felt connected to yourself the most. Where were you? What did that feel like?

___

___

___

CHAPTER 29

CONNECTING WITH OTHERS

sometimes,
you just have to listen
knowing you won't have
the answers
or be able to solve
their problems.
sometimes,
people just want to
be heard.
— y.c.

Connecting With Others Through Powerful Communication

Communication is an art and a dance. And communication isn't just about the words that are coming out of your mouth, but also how you get to *be* for another human being. And one way to do that is to align the intention of listening. In dancing, if you don't set the intention of that dance beforehand, such as if you're about to tango or salsa, with your dancing partner, then the dance wouldn't be as smooth and you might step on each others' toes! And just like dancing, if you don't agree on the intention of the specific communication that's about to take place, two people might metaphorically *step on each others' toes* during this dance of communication, relating and connecting. Here I present some practical tips on how to enhance your relating skills with others through intentional sharing and listening.

Two Ways to Actively Listen

There are masculine and feminine ways to be an active listener.

1. **Masculine** : Listening to help someone solve a problem
2. **Feminine:** Listening to create space for someone to just vent or open up

Often, miscommunication or conflicts occur when the intention of sharing and listening do not align due to lack of clarification.

Scenario 1:

Someone might be sharing just to express what they are experiencing, and the listener might listen actively and suggest solutions to fix the "problem." The sharing person, at this point, feels misunderstood because they were sharing a piece of them as they are, without needing to be "fixed." And while the listener *was* listening actively, because the intention was unclear, they didn't end up communicating effectively and missed an opportunity to create a healthy connection.

Scenario 2:

One person might be sharing in hopes of getting practical advice. When the listener doesn't offer any solutions, the sharer might feel the listener wasn't being present or engaging enough. A problem arises when the sharer doesn't let the listener know whether they want to tango or salsa, then becomes annoyed when the listener steps on their foot, not knowing what type of dance the sharer was intending at that moment.

Questions to Get on the Same Page

So how do you exactly check in to align the intentions of a sharer and a listener?

You can ask…

"Would you like me to listen and make space for you, or would you like me to help find a solution with you?" This question allows the other person to assess whether they are asking for masculine or feminine energy to show up in the conversation.

If they say, "I just want you to listen and I want to vent." Then you know that they are looking for connecting with you through sharing, feeling seen and accepted. You get to know that they don't want your input in *fixing* the problem. One thing you can do is set a specific duration where you are powerfully holding space for this person to vent. For example, in this case, you now get to say, "Got it. I am here for you to vent. For the next 10 minutes (you can pull out a timer) you have my undivided attention for you to vent."

If you ask, "Would you like me to listen and make space for you, or would you like me to help find a solution with you?" and they say, "I want you to help me find a solution. I need your advice." Then you know that now they are inviting your masculine listening to help them solve an issue at hand. In this case, these are the steps you get to take to create powerful connecting through communication.

First, listen to them. Then paraphrase back to them what you think you heard, and ask "is that a good summary of what you said? Is that right?" if the person says, yes, then you get to let them know, "Okay I have some ideas (or recommendations) for you. Are you open to my thoughts now?" Then, if they say yes, you get to now ensure that they are in a feedback or advice receiving mode. If they say no, then you get to hold space until you both get clear on what the problem is at hand first.

Sharer's Responsibility to Reveal Intention of Sharing

As the person sharing an experience, you can preface your intention of sharing by saying...

"So, I have something to share, and I'd love your ideas or feedback" (requesting "masculine" listening—to solve a problem).

or "I have something to share, and I appreciate you making space to let me vent" (requesting "feminine" listening/empathy and the space to be held for emoting and sharing).

You may be sitting there and thinking, this sounds like a way of communicating I've never done before! That's what most of my clients say when I coach them around this at first. What I find fascinating is that people would rather continue to communicate in ways that leave them with conflicts, miscommunication and misery, than try a different way of communicating that has shown to lead to clarity, harmony and therefore more effective connecting and relating with others. There's no right or wrong way to communicate; there are ways that can invite more clarity, connection, and working outcomes though. My invitation for you is, try it on! See what shifts for you when you try something different from your normal way of communication.

Connecting with Others Through Your Vibes

Dr. Bruce Lipton, a neuroscientist, says in one of his lectures titled "*Language Was Designed to Hide Vibrations*" he talks about how people can sense others' intentions through energy. He suggests each person has an energetic field that speaks before any specific words or language can, and it often speaks louder than actual words. Have you ever met someone whom you just felt had "good vibes" or "bad vibes"? Have you ever felt connected to someone, even if you haven't spoken many words with them? For instance, Dr. Lipton's example is of how a gazelle does not need to go "talk" to an animal like a lion, to figure out that they are not safe to be around.

And as we talked about before, the intention of how you want to show up for another human being is sometimes more meaningful than the actual words that are being said. And this is another reason that connecting to another human means that we get to do the inner work and commit to being a happy, conscious creature of our own. When we are happy and emit the radiance from genuine, deep fulfillment, then words don't have to say much for people to connect with you. They can feel good, comfortable and safe in your energy field.

Dr. Lipton's explanation may capture the essence of how we can already read people's vibes without specific language. I encourage you to do the Connecting Exercise below to understand this. It doesn't require any words. And this is really going back to why it is so powerful to be deeply fulfilled and genuinely happy in your life. When you commit to being genuinely happy in your life, you will find that you will naturally be more open for connection and therefore, it becomes easier to connect with others.

Connecting Exercise:

Ask someone to practice this connecting exercise with you. Let them know it will only take about five minutes.

1. With your partner or a friend with whom you want to deepen your connection, create a quiet space where there will be no distractions for the next few minutes.
2. Sit facing each other. Hold hands if you wish.
3. Each of you share your intention for this connecting exercise. It can be one word, such as "love" or "connection" or a full sentence.
4. Set a timer for four minutes. Start the timer.
5. Stare into each other's eyes for the next four minutes. This will be uncomfortable if you've never done it before. Just stay still, keep the eye contact, and allow whatever emotions that come up for you to come up.
6. After the four minutes, share what you observed about the other person.
7. Journal about the experience below.

____

____

____

CHAPTER 30

CONNECTING TO NATURE

I seek inspiration in nature,
and nature seeks inspiration in me.
Amongst the mutual flow of admiration,
we create, find beauty,
and love.
— y.c.

My Conversation with the Ocean

That morning, I realized how disconnected I've been feeling from my own soul. That day, I had been burying myself in my studio apartment in Newport Beach, where I listen to and learn from my mentors, training videos, and audiobooks, trying to fill my brain with as much information as possible. I was leading with this masculine energy of building, achieving, and succeeding. And although I would meditate every day for a few minutes, it was more to check it off from my to-do list than really connect with myself.

I woke up at 4:50 a.m., ready to take on the day and achieve, achieve, achieve—another day with masculine energy taking over. Then, as I was making coffee and going into "doing" mode, my lack of feminine energy hit me really hard, and I thirsted to connect with myself for a moment to find balance. So I changed my plans.

I put everything down. I left my cellphone at home and just started running toward the ocean.

I started running in silence—no audiobook, no music—to realize how much I haven't been listening to *me*, my own beautiful voice. I've bombarded myself with information and knowledge constantly, literally falling asleep listening to audiobooks, reading, taking in *so* much information. Yet I haven't let my soul and brain breathe to really listen to *me* and let the extended silence echo back to remind me of my own voice in a long time. *Well,* I thought, *I am so glad I am going for this run.* When I reached the sand at the beach, I climbed onto some big rocks to be close to the waves and the abundant ocean.

Wow. I forgot how hungry I was to connect with my soul and nature. I sat down on this big sturdy rock, still a little wet from the morning dew, and made myself comfortable for a meditation session. I started matching my inhales and exhales with the waves crashing and the tides coming in and out. I started to feel the breeze and the saltiness of the air tickle all my senses. Before I knew it, I fell into a deep, meditative state, and in my trance, I started a conversation with the ocean.

Me:

I am so thankful for you.

Your tides come in and out, matching my breathing, and I feel so connected to you. You remind me that you also breathe, just like me, and you are so alive.

These big rocks ground me; I love the weight you are able to share with me to create this stability and grounding.

Your waves crashing against these big rocks remind me of how courageous and majestic you are.

I can taste the saltiness of the air. It reminds me of my own tears I've tasted once, and it reminds me that you have the wisdom and depth to understand me.

You are so full of love, nurturing, and abundance, and I am so deeply thankful for you.

You are a healer. You are a nurturer. You are so beautiful.

Ocean:

So glad you're here. I've missed you.

Let me ask you, did you always feel that way about me?

Me:

No.

There were times in my life when things got really difficult, and I'd come visit you.

And your rocks felt cold.

You were so big, and I felt so small.

You seemed to carry on your days so majestically with or without me, and it felt lonely being in your big indifferent presence.

Ocean:

Have I changed?

Me:

No.

Ocean:

I've been doing this for thousands, millions of years. The changes I've experienced in the last few years or maybe decades that you've been even alive are minimal.

So what's the only thing that's changed?

Me:

Me…Me.

I've changed. I'm the only thing that's changed.

Ocean:

What you see in me is what you see in you.

What you see in others is what you see in you.

Right now, what you see is your own growth and change.

What you see is your own courage, your own beauty, your own majestic presence in your own being.

I am just a mirror.

I will be here as I am for a long time, and I will always be here to mirror you back to you.

I fell into tears, for this realization was so powerful, and I tasted the salty ocean on my lips as I opened my eyes.

And I said out loud before I started running back home, "Thank you. I will come back soon."

Exercise: Journaling

When was the last time you felt deeply connected to nature? Where were you and how did that connection to nature impact you? How does your connection to nature increase your happiness and peace in your life?

____

____

____

____

____

Chapter 31

Connecting to the Idea of Death

"I'd rather be dying"
brave me, for the End is known
Honesty and Truth have shifted from
luxuries to Reasons
Desires have weakened, yet
Intentions strengthened
Humbled, not afraid to
reveal my Vulnerability.
while imagining the eternal dark shadows of my eyelids
for the first time I
notice the different hues of the changing seasons,
the way the sun gracefully glides behind the twinkling horizon,
the delicate shape of the hidden tears and colorful laughter of those
I have loved, but never missed before.
the illusion of inching closer toward a known conclusion, rather than
moving away from the start
carves my greed down till I am left with
nothing,
but what I can bring to the gates of Heaven,
but haven't I always been moving in one direction
even before I left the innate warmth of the womb?
maybe

I'd rather be dying
than living.
— y.c.

Why does the realization that one will eventually die make it so much easier to motivate people to do what they really want to do to *live* his or her life? What would you do if you knew you only had… tomorrow, a week from now, a year, 5 years to live? Would that inspire you to live differently? Would that inspire you to live today differently? And what's truly stopping you from doing that *one* thing?

Lack of Growth = Dying

When I was working my last 9-5 corporate job, I felt stuck and I wasn't fulfilled because nothing was challenging me anymore. I felt as if I were slowly dying inside; I felt as if my soul was decaying with the absence of growth or that electric feeling of being alive. Have you ever felt this way?

I challenge you to think about this irony. That time between birth to death is sometimes called living and sometimes called dying. Living and dying are essentially the same journey towards the same direction. Realizing this, it became clear to me that even if I am technically alive, whether I am truly in the spirit living or in the spirit of dying each moment is really dependent on *how* I am spending that time. This deep realization freed me from my fear of death. I never have to be dying, if I choose to live intentionally and fully everyday instead. I can live fully every day, until my actual transition of my soul from this physical body, by doing things that excite my soul, by continuously challenging myself to grow, and by choosing into activities that light me up and help me feel alive. In this spirit, I would know that I am living to my fullest, and therefore, fear of death, which I believe is just fear of regrets and unknown, dissipates.

My Relationship with Death

"Why should a sunset be any less beautiful than a sunrise?" it read on a framed poster as I entered the hospice where my dad had been staying at.

His approaching end brought lots of tears to my eyes as I tried hard to find the beauty in it all, knowing and reminding myself that death is a natural cycle of life. I had been mentally preparing for my dad's passing, yet that day, all I could feel was shock, excruciating sadness, and emptiness.

My dad was a beautiful soul who fought cancer for 2.5 years like a warrior. He had been through *a lot* during those 2.5 years.

That September night, in 2017, he was noticeably more connected and energized than he had been in a few weeks. After the roller coaster of ups and downs with his health, seeing him even a few percentage better was such a celebration. That night, he reached for my and my mom's hands, and even gave us each a warm squeeze. He was having a difficult time breathing, but he was still telling me that I needed to eat and sleep well, and that I should go home and rest that night.

I typically headed home after he finished his dinners, but that night, my intuition told me to stay a little while longer. Still, I denied that this could be *the night* he would pass. About 1:40 a.m., I decided that even though my dad could not talk to me because all his energy went towards his breathing, I wanted to communicate with him. So I closed my eyes, hovered my hand above the left side of his bony rib cage, where his heart would be, and started matching his breathing to show him support and love. I wanted him to know I was there and wanted to be present with him. Even though I couldn't communicate with him verbally, I felt his energy and I felt connected to him. I can't really explain how I was able to feel all this just by breathing with him and hovering my hand over his heart, but I assure you I did. I was listening and talking to his soul, since his sick and broken body could not even allow him to speak properly anymore.

I meditated and prayed with him like that for a while. To my surprise, about 20 minutes of matching his breathing and hovering my hand over his heart, I felt that his energy was much calmer and more peaceful. I felt that he and I connected this way and he wanted me to go rest. So, I gave him one squeeze on his hand, kissed his hand and left. Then, I snuck out quietly around 2 a.m. so I could get some rest and be with him the next day.

Around 3:30 a.m.—I hadn't even been asleep for thirty minutes after getting home, my mom called to say I should return to the hospital. Exhausted and half-asleep, I said in my sleep, "Huh? I just got home from the hospital...." (I don't even remember this conversation - this is what my mom told me) and fell back asleep for five minutes. Then something *hit me awake*, and I woke up in a panic, realizing what that call probably meant. I looked at my mom's text. She said, "Drive safely and wear something warm."

I didn't even change. I left my apartment and anxiously drove back to the hospital. I was too exhausted and confused, or maybe too in denial, to realize what that call could actually mean. Twenty-five minutes of driving through the darkness outside, and I found myself at the hospital again. I had to ring the doorbell so a nurse could open the front door for me since it was 4:10 a.m., well before normal visiting hours.

I didn't run, but I walked fast, really fast. I nervously walked back into Room 36, where he had been staying for the last few weeks. I kept telling myself he is probably in a critical condition and I should prepare for the worst sometime within the next few days… but also, I had a heavy and cold feeling I could not explain.

As I walked into Room 36, my dad was already changed into nice white clothes and under clean white sheets. His IV and the air tube from his nose were gone. Then I immediately knew, before my mom could turn to me to speak with her broken heart and her red swollen eyes, "He left this world."

I felt every part of my body panic, and before I knew it, I was crying uncontrollably over his physical presence, but his spirit, his soul, his life had already left his body. His time of death was 3:58 a.m. The next few hours were a big blur—a nun from my mom's church came and said a prayer for him, and a few of my relatives came right away. Since he wished to donate his body to UCI for research, a few hours later, their representative came and picked up his body, and that was it. Just like that, he had gone to heaven and his body was also taken away.

*****

There's still parts of my heart that gets heavy describing that moment. It's been a few years now since my father passed away. You might wonder, why am I talking about death in a book about happiness? Why am I talking about a story that is "sad"? Why go into such details about it? Well, I believe getting present to the idea of death is one of the best ways to live as if every day is truly a gift... because we often forget. This was one of the most shocking as well as profound moments of my life. This was the moment I started to question what it really means to live. We often forget how precious life truly is. Here, I will share with you these lessons from experiencing death of a loved one, that actually helped me live a more powerful life.

No one's last breaths can be predicted, including yours. Within a few days of my dad's death, a mass shooting happened in Las Vegas. More than fifty people were killed without an opportunity to say goodbye to their loved ones. Some were young, some were older, yet no one expected they would die that night. You don't know when anyone's last day is. So live your best day today, everyday. Do life now. Live your life now. Be whoever you want to be *now.* Tell the people you love that you love them *today.* If you want to do something different in life, do it starting *today.* Stop waiting to do the things that are truly important to you in life. Fully cherish the gift of life and enjoy the delicious fruits of life as much as you can: joy, love, laughter, oneness, vulnerability and ease.

Death is, indeed, a natural part of life and teaches you impermanence.

I realized that many, if not most, people will go through the process of losing one of their parents or both parents during their lifetimes. Almost everyone is likely to lose *someone* they love within their lifetime. Death is a natural part of a human's (or any living thing's) life—yet it is often feared by many and a topic that is not talked about enough. In yoga, each yoga practice concludes with savasana (corpse pose). This corpse pose in the end serves as a powerful reminder of the impermanence of life. Death gives us the opportunity to truly celebrate the entire journey of life. That poster makes more sense to me now, "Why should a sunset be any less beautiful than a sunrise?" They are both natural and magnificent.

Wisdom, strength and even courage, are accessed after experiencing the death of a loved one.

As a child, one of my biggest fears was losing my parents. I had many nightmares about losing them when I was young. Experiencing my dad's passing reminded me that even when my biggest fear had come to reality yet I am here, I am still standing, and still living on, despite my worst case scenario actually coming to life. I, therefore, know today that I am far more resilient than I knew before, and my childhood fears are no longer valid now. I am more courageous, fearless, and wise because of it.

Grief is love.

If I hadn't met him and accepted him as my father (he was technically my stepdad but I treated him as my own dad from the time he married my mom when I was eleven), hadn't loved him deeply, and hadn't cultivated a strong daughter-father connection with him, I would not have felt grief. Grief exists because connection and love exist. Grief *is* love. All emotions are the energy of *love* manifesting in different forms.

Lastly, death makes the gift of life more valuable. Death is what makes each person's time on Earth a blessing, gives meaning, and makes life precious. I surrender to what I can't control, including that my dad has already passed. But I also pay extra attention to what I can control and how I can better myself and the world through the profound wisdom that surfaced from this experience. So what can I control? This includes how I choose to live each day. This includes the attitude that I get to hone into every moment. This includes being truly thankful for all that I have. This includes doing things that I am passionate about, even if it scares me. This includes choosing to create a life that I get to be proud of living and living courageously. And this is why understanding death is a crucial part when talking about the path towards true fulfillment and happiness. When you can get present to the idea of death, and the limited time we have on Earth, all the other things that we worried about or scared of naturally fall away. This gives you unlimited courage to live a life that you get to truly love.

Exercise

1. What is your current relationship with death? Get a pen and a piece of paper. Put a timer on for fifteen minutes, and answer these questions as a guideline. What do you think happens after death? What emotions come to you when you think about death? What close-to-death

experiences have you or other people in your life had? What did you learn in that process? Journal below.

2. How do you define dying vs. living?

3. If you are present to that you will die one day, what will you do today, that you've only been dreaming about?

CHAPTER 32

TRUSTING IN THE UNIVERSE: SURRENDERING

I used to not understand
how giving up and
surrendering were different.
but I get it now; giving up
means while I know I can,
I choose not to because it's just too hard.
surrendering is,
simply saying,
I trust you Universe, thank you,
for I know you will
take care of me.
today I surrender to all
that's good in this world.
— y.c.

Have you ever given your best to something but the result didn't turn out how you expected and found yourself feeling upset or angry? In those moments, how would it feel to lean in to trusting that the Universe is working for you, not against you instead? What would happen if you surrendered and let the Universe, Source, God, or your best self (or whatever you prefer calling the "divine being" as) provide you exactly what you need, at the right time, even if you don't know it at the time?

Oprah's Story on Surrendering

"I surrender all."

"I surrender all."

Oprah said that she started singing this, the moment she thought she lost the opportunity to star as *Sofia*, a leading role in her dream movie, based on her favorite book, *The Color Purple*. She talks about this surrender story in one of her Masterclasses (oprah.com). She had been obsessed with this book for many years, and she read the book countless times, she said. One day, as an aspiring actress, she hears that there is a movie being made about the book, and she was over the moon excited! She was convinced she would get the role of *Sofia,* the main character!

When she went to audition, she saw that in the movie script, one of the other characters' name was *Harpo*, which was her name spelled backwards! She thought, if that wasn't a sign she was supposed to get this job, what is?

Despite the signs, when she didn't hear back for a little while regarding the outcome of her audition and heard that a big-name movie star also auditioned for the same position, Oprah got discouraged. She decides that perhaps she is not meant for the role as she thought she was.

In despair, Oprah thought she was "too fat" to get the role, so she checked herself into a camp to lose weight. But then she realized that she couldn't stay in this despair forever. She decides to let go, trusting that everything is happening for a reason. That's when she started singing, "I surrender all." In the story she tells, Oprah says she was crying, it was pouring with rain, and she was soaked. She said she knew she had surrendered because she had reached the point of knowing even if someone else got the role, she would be genuinely happy for them. She found peace in her heart as she surrendered, knowing that she gave her best. That's when someone came after her, and said, "Oprah, there is a call for you!" To her surprise, Steven Spielberg was on the phone. He had personally called her to say, "You've got the role of Sofia; heard you're at a camp to lose weight. Make sure you don't lose one pound." She was confirmed perfect for the role after all.

The Color Purple ended up being the movie that kicked off Oprah's career as an actress allowing her to shine in her brilliance and led her to being the Oprah we know and admire today. Oprah says it was the moment she really surrendered that all her dreams came true. "God can dream a bigger dream for me, for you, than you could ever dream for yourself. When you've worked as hard and done as much and strived and tried and given and pled and bargained and hoped... surrender."

Formula for Surrendering

Surrendering is when your intention is set strongly, aligned with your best self, and when you have zero attachment to the outcome.

Surrendering =

Powerful intention set (aligned with your best self) --- attachment to outcome + complete faith in the Universe

Surrendering = Peace, Flow, Freedom

Surrendering to the highly intelligent power of the Universe allows us to cultivate the trust, or the faith, with the divine guidance of the Universe. This is when we can say, "Thank you, Universe. I am receiving your divine guidance and grateful that life is happening for me."

The beauty of surrendering is that the resistance and suffering vanishes away; then you can find yourself at peace. Then you can use the energy that you were using to have such a tight control over something that you didn't need to, and that can add to your ease instead. This ease is the divine breadcrumbs from the Universe; follow the ease. If you are not feeling good in your body, and it doesn't feel natural for you, consider a different way.

This is different from just giving up. It doesn't mean you just give up because something is hard to achieve. Surrendering is when you've done your absolute best, and things don't go *your way,* so you let the Universe lead the way. When you create more flow in your life this way, letting go of suffering, and you get to create space for more joy, fulfillment and peace in your heart.

Surrender Is a Form of Self-Love

Surrendering to the Universe is a work of self-love. When you surrender to the Universe, you let go of resistance, and you let go of suffering. And suffering is unnecessary. You lead yourself to loving yourself more this way as you create more space for flow and inner peace in your heart. Surrendering allows for you to get more out of the gifts the Universe has to offer. Surrendering is walking through life fearlessly without a worry, knowing that life will conspire for you in divine timing. So then you keep moving forward without heaviness. You keep moving forward being the light. You get to surrender knowing that you are taken care of. The Universe naturally keeps organizing itself for the highest good for all, beyond what we can comprehend and see from our perspective at times. So trust that.

Imagine that you are superman or super woman and you can fly out to space. Imagine that you try to stop the natural orbit and rotations of the Earth from orbiting the Sun. Imagine how much energy that would exhaust. Imagine even if you were semi-successful at slowing down that orbit for a bit, how would that throw off the order of all the other planets in our galaxy? Could that cause a clash and chaos for the rest of the Universe? What about the way the moon orbits the Earth? What would happen if you ever tried to stop it from moving in its natural orbital path so *you* could have more moonlight for a night, because you want the night to last longer just for you? What kind of confusion would that cause on the opposite side of the Earth by doing that?

Now, imagine that you, even despites your superpowers to fly and attempt to stop the planet from spinning, get out of the orbital path and let the Universe do its natural thing. How much easier would that be for you? How much easier would that be for the Earth? When it feels like when you're trying too hard to control how things go for things you don't have control over, let go. Get easy about it.

There is a natural force and order to the Universe that is not always readily visible with our own eyes, like the orbit of the moon and the orbit of the Earth. And there's an order to our everyday life that follows certain universal laws that aren't always readily visible to our eyes; but when this natural order is not honored, it can cause more conflicts and chaos than necessary. The natural flow of life is ease. In the awareness of unnatural resistance, after you've given your best, remember to try surrendering, and let the Universe unfold its magic for you.

"I am so grateful that surrender had taught me to willingly participate in life's dance with a quiet mind and an open heart."

- Michael A. Singer, *The Surrender Experiment*

Exercise

What have you been resisting, instead of surrendering?

____

____

____

____

____

____

CHAPTER 33

OWNING YOUR SPIRITUALITY

Let your faith
guide the way.
Let your faith
be the magnet
for all your blessings.
— y.c.

I just blurted out, "Dr. Luévano, I am confused," and my eyes started to tear up. I was overwhelmed. My college World Religion Professor, who was also a Catholic Priest, took off his glasses, leaning in, and readjusted his body to give me full attention. "What are you confused about dear?" Back in 2007, I walked into my professor's office at Chapman University. As I sat in front of him, I started welling up with tears before I could even speak.

"I grew up really Catholic since I was born," I started to share. "I was so committed to being Catholic for a while. But since then, I have been distancing myself from church because I am confused about my religion and the things I learned as a Catholic. And sometimes I feel guilty about it. And I really miss church, and I really miss having that religious foundation."

"What happened that caused you to distance yourself?" he asked.

"Well, I will just say it. First of all, some of my friends are gay. I cannot accept that the church rejects them" (back in 2007, it was still illegal for gay people to get married in most states, and discrimination was even worse than it is now.) and I continued,

"And… someone close to me attempted suicide a few years ago. My mom and dad, and plenty of other people I love got divorced. I am confused because I feel like being a Catholic means I have to live with the fact that some of these people I love are not accepted by the Church and maybe even go to hell. And I know that's not true. People try to take their lives because they are suffering. Divorces happen because people's directions in their lives change. And I don't think there's anything wrong with being gay. But without having a "religion" to fall back on, I wonder what my moral foundation is. I know I have one, but it doesn't fit into my religion."

At this point, I was crying. I had never told anyone that before. I was scared he would judge me. I was scared he would say I am a sinner, too, for not being committed to being a good Catholic.

He said, "Yuri, modern Catholicism accepts all people. Catholicism believes in love like all religions. And you don't have to be Catholic to be a good, loving human. You can find god anywhere."

I looked up, puzzled, wiping tears off my eyes. "What do you mean?" I asked.

"You don't have to be religious to believe in God," he said. "You don't have to be Catholic to be spiritual or religious. God loves you."

At this point, I was even more confused. I was not expecting this coming from a Catholic priest.

"What do you mean?"

"Just work on building your spiritual foundation, whatever serves you. Whatever is closest to God, and to love."

That day changed the way I relate to spirituality forever. He gave me the invisible permission slip to free myself from feeling trapped in a religion. He reminded me I can believe in the force of love and God, in my own way. And as for me, that day, my spiritual journey started as I started to build my own building blocks for my own unique spiritual path.

For the first few years of my search towards my spiritual foundation over a decade ago, I tried on lots of different ideas, through the process of trial-and-error. In this process, I started to create my own moral system, starting with basic level beliefs such as stealing is bad, helping is good, ditching class when there is a test is bad, drinking and driving is bad, and such. Over the years, this foundation became less superficial and more expansive, and I started to see the important values hidden within those distinctions that I truly honored. I realized then too, that being spiritual didn't mean fearing doing things that are "bad." It was rather about the practice of fine tuning into a life that aligns with the most divine version of myself everyday as best as I can. And that it was about being the force of love. So, I started to see how helping others, searching for ways to self-improve, finding purpose all tied into this.

Then I discovered yoga and yogic philosophy when I started to go through my 200-hour Registered Yoga Teacher Training at Corepower Yoga. Learning about the Eight Limbs of Yoga, I found exactly what I was looking for: a set of life guidelines that did not judge anyone and felt inclusive to everyone! They were the Yamas & Niyamas. They are basically the 10 commandments of yogic philosophy, that included concepts such as non-violence *(ahimsa)*, truth (*satya*), non-stealing (*asteya)*, moderation (*brahmacharya)*, non-envy (*aparigraha*), purity (*sauca)*, contentment (*santosha*), surrender (*ishvara pranidhana*), discipline (*tapas)* and study of self (*svadhyaya)*. These yogic guidelines became my new building ground for my new spiritual path for the next decade and beyond. Then over time, my natural curiosity drew me to learning more about all different kinds of religion and philosophies, from various spiritual leaders and teachers, and from my own experiences. I studied and adopted some wisdom from Buddhism that resonated with me, such as its teachings of deep compassion and love. I was thankful for Catholicism for allowing me to build my initial foundation in spirituality and allowing me to learn at an early age that I could communicate to divinity through prayers. I was fascinated and moved by the Hindus' and their belief that everything has a soul (and much of yoga is derived from Hindu traditions). I loved learning from modern day spiritual leaders, such as *Abraham-Hicks* and its channeled messages of laws of attraction. I studied Ancient Egyptian Hermetic Mysticism. The universal laws that govern the Universe according to these philosophies especially deeply impacted me. Over time, I realized that they all had a few common themes. While impossible to simplify in one sentence, or even in one chapter or a book, I can say these few words to sum up my spiritual foundation: we are meant to live leading with love, gratitude, and laughter, we are all deeply connected, we all have souls within our bodies, and we are miracles with infinite potential to create our reality. My continuous spiritual practice is to go back to these few governing foundations everyday more and more and evolve as a soul in that process.

In this book, we explored many ways to live with more joy and peace, and in that, we explored ways to be more spiritually evolved, whether you knew it or not. These concepts are parallel. For example, accessing your creativity and honoring your expression are your spiritual practices. Asking yourself why you're here on Earth and starting to unapologetically live out your purpose are the initial stages of your spiritual awakening. Managing and understanding your emotions and allowing them to guide you in your journey is your practice of learning more about your soul. Your commitment to live being more present is your commitment to your spiritual path. Empowering the creator within you and committing to live with pure joy are the celebration of your spiritual self. And we can even consider our "negative" experiences or emotions as spiritual, as they offer the very lessons that redirect us back towards our spiritual path and who we really are. In fact, every human experience is a spiritual experience.

Remember from the beginning of the book, I reminded you that you are a miracle. I reminded you that you had one in many trillion chances of being born. You existing on this beautiful planet with all the abundant resources for you to live and experience today, is in fact, the most miraculous incidence. And when we get to remember this as a foundation of our everyday living, in all moments, we can choose to find gratitude and peace. While this book offered you many practical exercises and different perspectives for you to try on to ignite your own path to happiness, long-term, eternal inner peace and fulfillment only co-exist when one commits him or herself to cultivating a spiritual relationship. And remember that as a creator, you can also develop your own foundation of spirituality that makes sense for your soul. There is no right or wrong, good or bad ways to *be spiritual.* You are already spiritual, whether you like it or not. However, I invite you to dive deeper into creating a spiritual relationship, any kind of relationship, to something bigger, more magnificent than you in human form, like the Universe, God, the Source, your most divine self, or whatever you want to call it, and devote time and energy to that relationship for unshakable peace and deep fulfillment. And one way to start, is to simply become aware, and start to ponder about your relationship to spirituality *without judgement.*

And on that note, as nothing is an accident, I am very grateful that the Universe brought you and I together here and right now. Many of my clients have told me in the past, "I felt very pulled to work with you, and I can't really explain it!" And in that, I just smile and say, "Yes, I have absolute faith that the Universe brought us together here for a reason. We have some work to do!" as I kick off my coaching journey with them. And for the same reason, I have absolute faith that the Universe brought you to these words on these pages for us to meet this way, and it was an honor to guide you and connect with you through this book. Thank you for existing and thank you for meeting me here. You are truly miraculous and it's an honor to co-create on this planet as we all expand ourselves towards living our best versions of ourselves towards joy and peace.

Concluding Prayer:

Dear Universe (or God, or the divinity you resonate with),

I hereby request your divine guidance as I commit to living as a powerful creator that I am.

I hereby request your divine guidance as I commit to living as a powerful manifestor that I am.

I hereby request your divine guidance as I commit to creating my own happiness and honoring all aspects of my journey.

I hereby request your divine guidance as I commit to living as a peaceful being.

I celebrate my existence as it truly is a miracle.

I cherish my ability to love unconditionally and show up authentically to this world.

Thank you, Universe, for all the blessings and the lessons that have unfolded throughout this book and in my life.

I am grateful to know that I am infinitely loved and supported.

I thank you, I thank you, I thank you, Universe.

"True freedom is always spiritual.
It has something to do with your innermost being,
which cannot be chained, handcuffed, or put into a jail."
— Osho

Journaling Exercise: What is your relationship and story to your spirituality? What is your relationship to the Universe?

A FINAL NOTE

Now that you have read and finished this book, I hope you get a chance to start your own journey towards redefining your own relationship to yourself, the Universe, and your perspective on a happy life. While learning and exploring these concepts happiness can be a great start, it is not until one starts to take inspired and dedicated actions towards their best self that actually creates a transformation. So I am curious; after reading this book, what were you inspired to take immediate action on? Starting your own business? Writing your own book? Creating more fulfilling relationships? Making your happiness and health your priority? Are you looking to apply what you know to become a better version of yourself and finally let go of some of your toxic habits that don't align with who you want to become? What new possibilities are and have started to emerge for you reading this book? Journal Below.

The new possibilities I'd like to create in my life aligned to my best self are:

____

____

____

____

____

____

Congratulations on creating these new possibilities! What 5 inspired actions can you start taking today towards your best, most divine, joyful self? What areas of your life are you truly committed to changing? What will that do for you, the rest of your life, the people in your life, and everyone in the world? How will stepping up to be the best version of yourself start to shift the world around you? When you commit to this path of transformation, what do you think could happen? I've learned over the years of reading many books that I can read all the books in the world, but my actual transformation came only from putting in the inner work and taking different sets of actions for a period of time and staying accountable to it. So I invite you to declare now, and powerfully! What new inspired actions are you committed to as a result of reading this book?

Below, list 5-10 action items you commit to in the next 90 days:

(i.e. quit smoking, get a gym membership, stick to a morning routine, meditate daily, hire a coach, create a website for your dream business, write a book, create a course, etc.)

1. ______________________________

2. ______________________________

3. ______________________________

4. ______________________________

5. ______________________________

6. ______________________________

7. ______________________________

8. ______________________________

9. ______________________________

10. ____

If you feel called to do so as you write out some exciting new possibilities inspired from reading this book, I'd like to invite you to share these with me by emailing me or visiting my website. It would be an honor to connect with you. Also, if there is anything that deeply resonated with you, or something that could be improved, I would appreciate your feedback as well for my continued growth. Also, I'd love to learn more about you, your challenges, your obstacles, and your adversities, and see how I can potentially serve you as you as your coach and mentor. In fact, I would like to offer you a complimentary, 15-minute consultation by phone, Zoom, or in person (if geography allows) to see how I can help and assist you, if you feel inspired to do so.

My email address is: coachwithyuri@gmail.com. Feel free to email with your name and time zone and we will schedule your complimentary consultation. Meanwhile, I am sending you so much light and love. I wish you abundance, happiness, joy, and prosperity!

With Infinite Gratitude,

Yuri Choi

About the Author

Yuri Choi is a best selling author, coach, YouTuber, and a keynote speaker. She is the Founder of *Yuri Choi Coaching* and she helps high performers and entrepreneurs create powerful results and fulfillment through helping them create and stay in a powerful, abundant and unstoppable mindset to achieve their goals and create a life they love.

Yuri is actively booking stages, both in person and virtual, and she is passionate about spreading the messages about mindfulness, power of intention, and creating a powerful mindset to live a fulfilling life. She is also the designated mindset coach for the largest online magazine and mental health YouTube channel, *Psych2Go*, and offers virtual workshops for their 8 million subscribers. She is also a Habitude Warrior Conference MC and Rockstar Speaker. Yuri is also a co- author of the best selling book series, *13 Steps to Riches: Habitude Warrior*, for *Faith* and *Desire* editions. In the series, she collaborates with Sharon Lechter, Denis Waitley, John Assaraf, Erik Swanson, Kevin Harrington and others.

Yuri Choi has served as an active leader of a leadership group to generate the efforts of a special initiative charity called Frontline Hero Fund (frontlineherofund.org), raising over $150,000 for COVID-19 positive frontline heroes and their families in critical conditions or those who passed away in 2020. She's also been volunteering in the volunteer exec committee for the *American Foundation for Suicide Prevention* for several years to eliminate stigma around mental health, raise funds and to contribute to the efforts to eliminate suicide.

Yuri stays open to opportunities to support causes around mental health, creating solutions for homelessness, and promoting mindfulness.

Yuri was originally born in South Korea, and she is a first-generation immigrant and currently back in sunny Southern California, after living and exploring in Seoul, Korea for the last year. Yuri is also a yogi, artist, poet and lifelong learner. She loves to play and learn the piano and the guitar, and go on adventures with her friends when she is not serving and coaching her clients, writing books, creating videos, at events, or doing workshops.

To find the author on different platforms, feel free to check out YuriChoiCoaching.com as well as her YouTube Channel (YouTube.com/c/yurichoi). To connect with her and follow her on Instagram, her handle is @yuri1c (instagram.com/yuri1c). To contact Yuri Choi directly, feel free to reach out to her at creatingyourownhappiness.com or email her at coachwithyuri@gmail.com.